AF604225

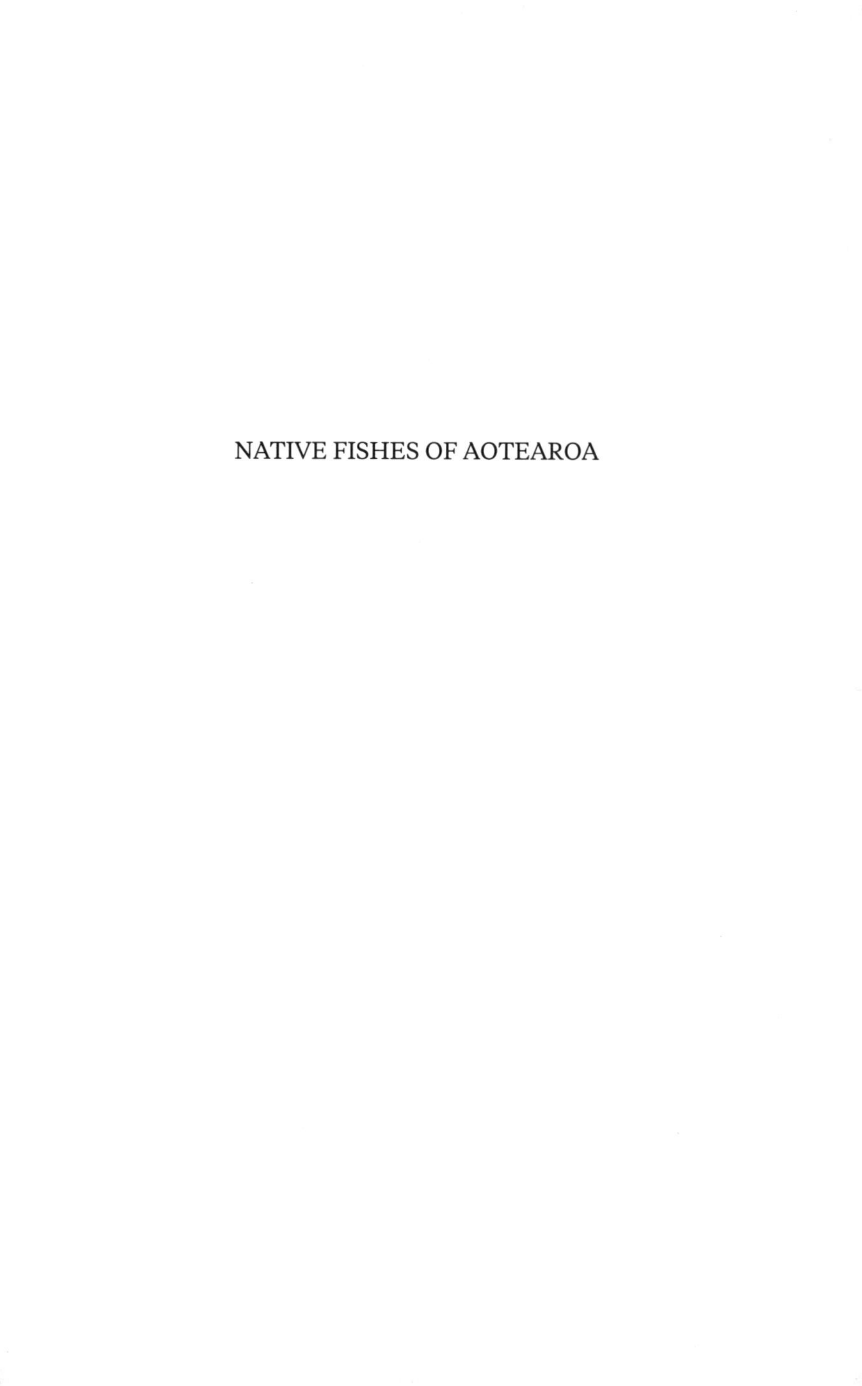

NATIVE FISHES OF AOTEAROA

ALSO IN THIS SERIES

Native Birds of Aotearoa

Native Plants of Aotearoa

Native Insects of Aotearoa

Native Shells of Aotearoa

Native Spiders of Aotearoa

NATIVE FISHES OF AOTEAROA

Andrew Stewart

CONTENTS

Introduction 7
Classifying and identifying fish 11
About this book 14
The fishes 17
Glossary 140
References and further reading 143
Acknowledgements 144
Index of species 145
About the author 150
About the illustrators 150

INTRODUCTION

Directly or indirectly, water influences everything in Aotearoa New Zealand. We are surrounded by ocean, and water-based activities of all kinds are extremely popular. Sea temperatures drive much of our weather. Large rivers bisecting the country significantly challenge movement, so much so that drowning while trying to cross a river has been called 'the New Zealand death'. Our seafood industry earns tens of millions of dollars each year and employs hundreds of New Zealanders. The ability to go down to the sea and 'catch a feed' is part of our national psyche. Children of all ages catch either a yelloweye mullet or a spotty as their first fish.

For early Māori, the absence of large land mammals and the loss of moa and other birds meant that fishes rapidly became a vital source of protein and, in the case of freshwater eels, fats. Coming from the Pacific islands, Māori were already adept at catching fish and harvesting shellfish. Detailed protocols were established to ensure that stocks were well managed.

The fishes we have here in Aotearoa are the result of 100 million years of dynamic geology and climate. As the land split off from Gondwana and plate tectonics began to push us further eastwards into the Pacific Ocean, the recruitment of species from our larger neighbours became more and more difficult. Further plate tectonics caused the land to submerge and then re-emerge. Plates grinding against each other thrust up mountain ranges, and volcanoes spluttered into life. Coupled with multiple dramatic global climate swings from ice ages to warming, the slate of life was repeatedly wiped clean. This led to opportunities for those hardy generalists that survived to evolve to occupy vacant real estate. As a result, endemism in the fishes of Aotearoa is extremely high, approaching 20 percent; and the triplefins (also known as 'cockabullies') are now recognised as one of the rare examples of a marine species flock – where there is an evolutionary explosion of closely related species that colonise empty habitats.

Aotearoa today straddles a wide latitude both geographically and politically, from Rangitāhua Kermadec Islands to the north, Rēkohu Wharekauri Chatham Islands to the east and the islands on the Campbell Plateau to the south. Geographically, we also sit at the junction of influence from three oceans: the Pacific, the Indian and the Southern. The two main islands are long and thin, situated across warm-temperate to cool-temperate waters. The subtropical front sweeps east around the bottom of Te Waipounamu South Island, and the Tasman Front brings warm water to Te Tai Tokerau Northland. The Antarctic Circumpolar Current breaks the Deep Western Boundary Current off to pass around the eastern boundary of Aotearoa and up through the Kermadec Trench. The average depth of New Zealand's Exclusive Economic Zone (EEZ) is around 2000m. The region holds the fifth-deepest trench (the Kermadec) in the world, which bottoms out at around 10,000m. The submarine geology is also complex, with thousands of seamounts and five ridges radiating out from northern Te Ika-a-Māui North Island like fingers on a hand.

Recently published research has uncovered the presence of our planet's seventh continent, Zealandia, the size of North America and of which Aotearoa is the part above sea level. Although over 1400 fish species have been identified throughout this region, the marine fishes selected for this book are those found much closer to home, around the coastal shelf, defined as from the low-tide line to the shelf break at about 200m depth.

Freshwater fishes are strongly represented, with hundreds of creeks, streams, rivers and lakes of all sizes across the motu. These host the largest number of galaxiid species in the world, along with 'bullies' and the iconic freshwater eels. Along with the eels, some of the galaxiids are migratory, running to sea to spawn or grow and returning as 'whitebait'; while other galaxiids are land-locked. The same pattern is seen in the freshwater bullies.

Our freshwater fishes were originally considered to be poor in terms of size and edibility, so non-native fishes were introduced by European settlers. Introduced salmonids, especially, have become extremely popular for recreational fishing, as well as a highly profitable food industry. The knock-on effect of this, though, has been to the detriment of our native species. Sadly, we seem to have realised too late that the species we do have, while not necessarily big and flashy, are unique and worthy of protection. Even among the native species, all too often edibility is still seen as the principal driver; eels and whitebait being of first importance. The extinction of the native 'grayling' upokororo stands as a symbol of both our hubris and our ignorance of our fresh waters.

Early Pākehā researchers struggled to understand the level of unique fauna in Aotearoa. Arriving with a Eurocentric worldview, they tended to believe that many of the fishes they were seeing were the same as the species they were familiar with in 'the old country'. This is reflected in some of the common names still used today: 'smelt' (it's not a true smelt) and 'blue cod' (it's nowhere close to a true cod). As a result, many of the lists published early on include names that we cannot reliably associate with the species we know today. Another factor in this was the challenge of disseminating information.

Even over the 40 or so years of my own work in the field, technology has hugely improved the ability to share knowledge around the world. From writing out and posting letters then waiting for months for a reply, to instant electronic communication of documents and images around the world, technology has improved our understanding of the natural world.

It is my dearest hope that we reverse the destruction and loss of aquatic habitats, so that my grandchildren and their grandchildren will enjoy the fresh water and marine world, discovering their wonders as I did. As the common saying goes, 'We do not inherit the Earth from our ancestors; we borrow it from our children'.

THE FISH COLLECTION AT TE PAPA

As the national museum, Te Papa is charged under the Museum of New Zealand Te Papa Tongarewa Act 1992 to hold the National Fish Collection – the largest collection of preserved fish specimens in Aotearoa. The scope of the collection covers, in order of importance:

1. The land, EEZ and Extended Continental Shelf (ECS) of Aotearoa;
2. The Ross Dependency;
3. The wider Pacific and Southern Oceans.

To that end, at the time of writing we hold over 240,000 specimens in nearly 63,000 lots. These are kept in about 42,000 jars (70ml to 2L), 1200 drums of 20L, and 158 stainless steel tanks (250 to 3300L). This last is the largest collection of big fish specimens in the world. The oldest specimen in the collection is a hoki caught in Te Whanganui-a-Tara Wellington Harbour in 1869. The physical collection is supported by an extensive library of books and scientific publications dating back to 1735.

Specimens are mostly stored in a solution of alcohol, and in a specialised facility that keeps them at a constant temperature and humidity. The large numbers and sizes mean that we can acquire good data on the range of variation that naturally occurs in a species (juvenile to adult, male and female) as opposed to the differences between species. They also act as a snapshot in time and space, a permanent record of what species lived where. This is becoming more important, as global warming is causing species to shift to ensure they are living in their optimal temperature band.

Identification and new species descriptions are the traditional roles of a museum. The science of describing new species is called taxonomy, and, paradoxically, although the calls on our skills are increasing, the teaching of this science at universities is now almost non-existent.

Taxonomic research on fishes at Te Papa has tended to focus on the marine fauna, ranging from the triplefins living in intertidal rockpools to the inhabitants of deep offshore regions, seamounts and ridges. Many areas are still unexplored; the three-week-long 2016 Kermadec Expedition alone caught over 30 new records for the region as well as several rare and new species. The vast mid-water regions of the EEZ are under-sampled, if at all. The biggest challenge here is the cost of getting to areas and being able to conduct sampling in waters with an average depth of 2000m – the deeper you go, the more expensive the work becomes. However, that isn't really an excuse. As we have declared a 200-nautical-mile EEZ, it behoves us to know what is there. Closer to home, several land-locked galaxiid species in the Ōtākou Otago region still require formal description. Scientifically, the only valid way to achieve this is with specimens that are properly curated and kept in an accessible collection facility. New genetic techniques, notably DNA, are increasingly used but this also needs to be supported by voucher specimens (preserved specimens archived in a permanent collection), that give confidence in the identification and can be checked and re-checked as necessary.

The late Bob McDowall was the internationally accepted expert on the freshwater taxa, especially the galaxiids (pages 125–31), and his work covers the freshwater regions of Aotearoa. After his untimely passing, the extensive collection he had inherited and amassed at the National Institute of Water and Atmospheric Research (NIWA) centre in Christchurch was deposited into the collection at Te Papa.

Andrew Stewart

CLASSIFYING AND IDENTIFYING FISH

WHAT IS A FISH?

At first glance, this seems a rather obvious question; everyone knows what a fish is. However, defining *exactly* what defines the creatures we call fish becomes as slippery as the animal itself. Every time a description or definition is put forward there are numerous exceptions, often muddied by some of the other vertebrates, especially amphibians. Genetics has also revealed what many suspected all along: that all vertebrates, including humans, are 'fish'. Kahawai are more closely related to humans than to sharks, and sharks are more closely related to us than to hagfish. Even something as basic as being cold-blooded is challenged by discoveries about heat production and retention in diverse groups such as the mako shark, tuna, and opahs (e.g. moonfish). The late ichthyologist Joe Nelson defined it most succinctly in his book *Fishes of the World:* a fish is 'an aquatic vertebrate with gills throughout all its life, and with limbs (when present) in the shape of fins' (Nelson, 1994).

The word 'fish' comes from the Old English *fisc*, whose exact meaning has been lost in the mists of time. Hence it is attached to a host of animals that do not have any relationship with what this book covers: these include starfish, jellyfish, crayfish and even blackfish (pilot whales). Using Nelson's definition, fishes are the dominant vertebrate group on the planet, with over 33,000 species. This is more than the number of amphibians, reptiles, birds and mammal species combined, and there are many more to be found. The isolated fresh waters are evolutionary laboratories, and the deeper reefs beyond normal SCUBA depths are revealing more and more new species. Genetic analysis is also uncovering that some species previously thought to be widespread are in fact several similar-looking species.

Another question many people have is whether to use 'fish' or 'fishes' for the plural. Both are correct, though it depends on the number of species being discussed. If there is only one species, then the plural is fish. If there are more than one species, then fishes is used – hence the title of this book.

BASIC FISH AND RAY ANATOMY

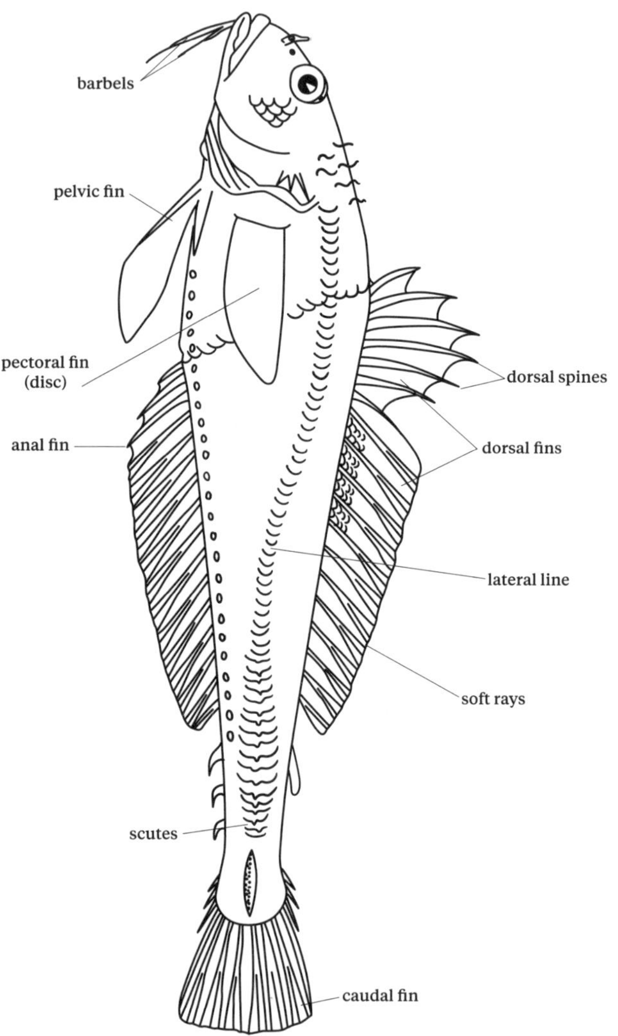

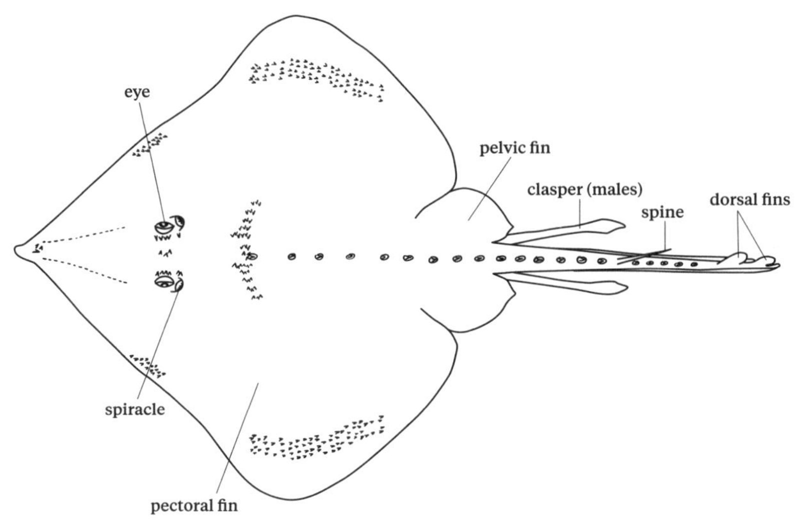

STANDARD UNITS OF MEASUREMENT

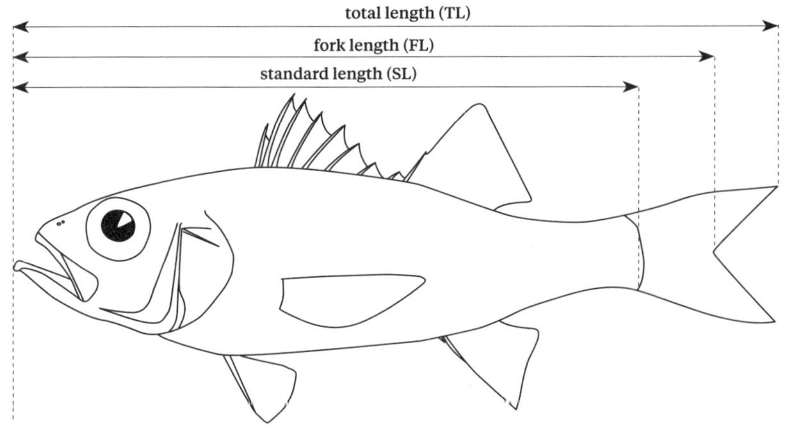

ABOUT THIS BOOK

This book is a successor to the small 1949 Nature in New Zealand series guide published by AH & AW Reed, specifically *Native Fishes* by WJ Phillipps, who was Ichthyologist at the Dominion Museum (1917–58).

With over 1400 species of fishes now known from our EEZ, and many more expected to be found and described, the challenge was which ones to choose for this book. Selection was made on the basis of the likelihood of being encountered by people who purchased this book. For this reason, you will not find some of our more exotically named deeper-water residents such as spookfish, cagemouth and periscope eel.

The te reo names and English common names are dominant, reflecting the intended audience. Scientific names follow those used in *The Fishes of New Zealand* (Te Papa Press, 2015); these names are used to order the species, but the final arrangement in this book reflects the more radical order that molecular analysis has created over the decade since that publication appeared.

Māori names were derived from Rowan Strickland's 1990 *Nga tini a Tangaroa: A Maori–English, English–Maori dictionary of fish names.* At the point of first European contact with tangata whenua, it was noted that Māori had names for all the fishes, large and small. Regrettably, the collision of cultures saw Māori knowledge, being orally transmitted, shed; much of it was lost before it could be recorded. This is evident in Strickland's publication, where there are over 170 te reo entries recorded as just 'Fish' for the English name.

As acute observers of their environment, Māori would have applied names to different species and recognised distinct sizes, stages and sex. It is also inconceivable that they were not aware of the small rockpool fishes as well as larger species such as the southern bastard cod, giant boarfish and scorpionfish, all of which have no recorded te reo names. Conversely, the Māori names of some fish have become the standard in Aotearoa, such as moki, parore and kahawai. As a living language, this imbalance is starting to be redressed with new names being coined to reflect the bicultural aspirations of the country. As official languages of the motu, place names recorded herein include both the te reo Māori and English names.

Each species has an illustration and a physical description. Descriptions are generalised and simplified; they include details relevant to identification, including colour, but these are not comprehensive as the illustrations speak for themselves. Readers can also refer to some of the common body parts labelled on pages 12–13 and to the glossary at the end of the book, particularly for descriptions of caudal fin shapes, which cannot be easily simplified. Additional comments on distribution and habitat include relevant notes on endemism and any other details about the fish's appearance, lifecycle, diet or behaviour. Because most readers will have primarily encountered fishes as a food source, comment is made on the species' eating quality, where appropriate.

The illustrations in this book are by specialist fish illustrators Helen Casey, Michelle Freeborn, Erica MacKay and Bob McDowall (see pages 150–51). With the exception of McDowall, they were commissioned by Te Papa. The illustrations are pen and ink on heavy paper and are based on proportional measurements scaled to a standard size. The rough sketch is first done using a soft pencil before setting permanently with Indian ink. Colour patterns and shading to give a 3D effect is achieved by stippling.

The internationally accepted style of illustrations is to have the fish with its head facing left, an exception being the right-eyed flounders which are depicted with the head facing right. This format allows for illustrations to be directly compared with each other. For space reasons, most of the illustrations in this book are shown with the head at the top, likewise allowing direct comparison.

THE FISHES

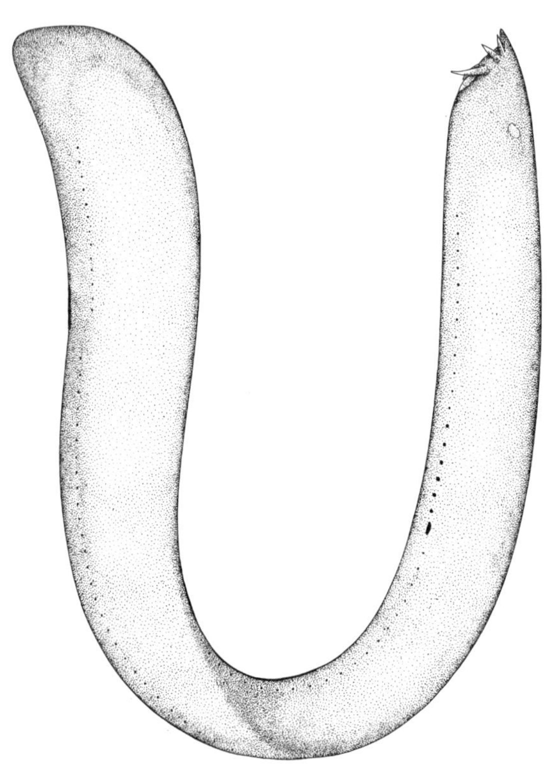

NAPIA, PIA, TUARE, TUERE
CRYPTIC HAGFISH

Eptatretus cryptus

Description: The cryptic hagfish has a pale to mid-brown, elongated, eel-shaped body, with a cylindrical head and flattened tail. The head is distinguished by a short tube for a nostril, five pairs of short barbels around the snout and mouth, and a pair of off-white eyespots. It has seven branchial openings and a line of 75–98 slime pores from the head onto the tail. A small fin fold runs along the bottom of the trunk. It has been recorded as reaching 97cm total length.

Distribution in Aotearoa: An endemic species, occurring from off Otou North Cape to southern Ata Whenua Fiordland and east to off Rēkohu Wharekauri Chatham Islands.

Habitat: Coastal down to over 900m depth in association with reefs and shelly sediment.

Curator's notes: This species is difficult to separate from the common hagfish. There are modal differences in the head slime pore counts (12–15, usually 14, for the cryptic compared with 15–18, usually 16, for the common hagfish), and the common hagfish has at least some slime pores with fine, white rims. The hagfish family is unique among vertebrates in their ability to produce a fine silk-like thread up to 70 percent of the tensile strength of spider's silk. Eight hagfish species are found around the New Zealand coastline, some with striking patterns and colours. Included is the world's largest and heaviest species, the Goliath hagfish, which grows to over 6kg in weight. Many of the larger specimens are caught and exported to Asia for their meat, and the skin, which is processed into high-quality leather (marketed as 'eel skin'). Aotearoa is one of the few places in the world where hagfishes can be seen at snorkelling depths.

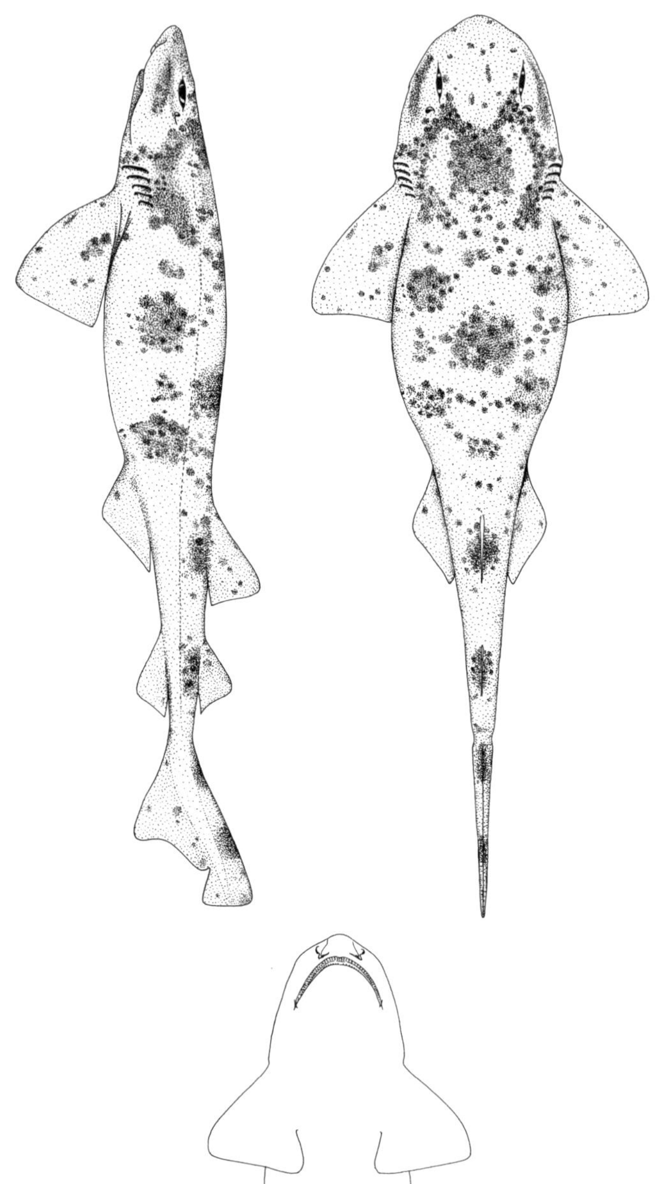

PEKAPEKA
CARPET SHARK

Cephaloscyllium isabellum

Description: The pekapeka is brown with an off-white belly, several dark spots and saddles over the body, and two dark bars across the tail. Its head is small yet broad. A large mouth extends back beyond the eyes and contains small, pointed teeth like coarse sandpaper. The eyes are small and oval. The two dorsal fins are bluntly angular, with the first over the pelvic fins and the second over the anal fin. The caudal fin is elongate with lobes forming a D-shape. It has rough skin with large erect denticles (tooth-like scales). Females grow much larger than males, up to 90cm total length.

Distribution in Aotearoa: An endemic species, found from Otou North Cape to Rakiura Stewart Island and Wharekauri Rēkohu Chatham Islands.

Habitat: Coastal in 0–700m depth, being more common on sandy to shelly-cobble bottoms.

Curator's notes: Females can lay up to 14 eggs, each with a single embryo. Egg cases are attached to kelp or sponges with long threads off the ends. Empty cases that sometimes wash ashore are called 'mermaid's purses'. Rising sea temperatures are putting this shark at risk, as the young in the eggs often do not develop in warmer water. Being slow swimmers, pekapeka are easily caught by hand on SCUBA. When caught, they will stiffen and curl up, swallowing sea water to try to appear bigger to predators. This shark is most active at night, when it feeds on small animals living in and on the sea bed. The carpet shark was the first New Zealand fish to be scientifically described, in 1788.

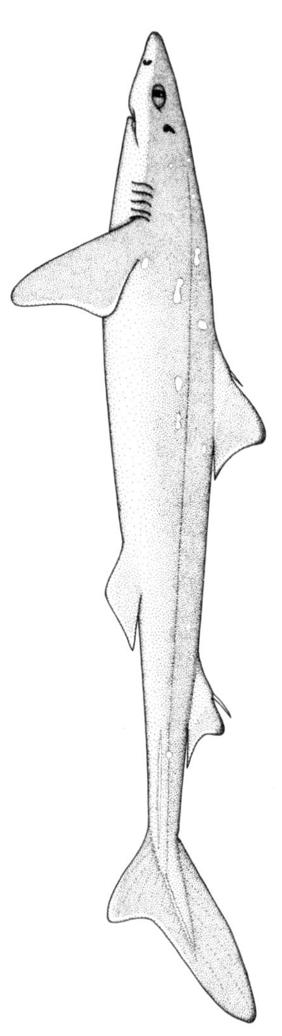

KOINGA, MANGŌ-HAPŪ, MANGŌ-PEKEPEKE

SPINY DOGFISH

Squalus acanthias

Description: Mid-grey to brown-grey above with a white belly and white spots over the flanks and upper body, this slender shark has a pointed snout overhanging the mouth. The eyes are oval. The teeth are small, flattened and blade-like. The two dorsal fins are large and pointed, with the first positioned about mid-body and larger than the second, both with a strong, sharp curved spine. There is no anal fin. The skin is silky to the touch with small denticles. Males can grow up to 90cm total length and females are at least 1m larger.

Distribution in Aotearoa: Found around Aotearoa, being more common in the south, onto the Campbell Plateau and around Rēkohu Wharekauri Chatham Islands; also globally in cool water off Greenland, southern South America, southern Africa and southern Australia. The spiny dogfish is listed as vulnerable by the IUCN, although its status in Aotearoa is Not Threatened.

Habitat: Found from the surface to the sea bed, being more common in surface waters at night. They have been caught at depths of up to 1446m.

Curator's notes: Dogfishes often school in same-sex groups. Females carry the young for almost two years and can produce up to 16 pups. Pregnant females will often birth their pups when caught. A long-lived species, spiny dogfish have been estimated to live to almost 70 years, with some estimates of 100 years. When removing one from the hook, never hold it just behind the head as they can curl right around and stab with their second dorsal fin spine, causing a painful wound that is slow to heal. Instead, curl the tail around and secure it against the side of the head to immobilise the shark.

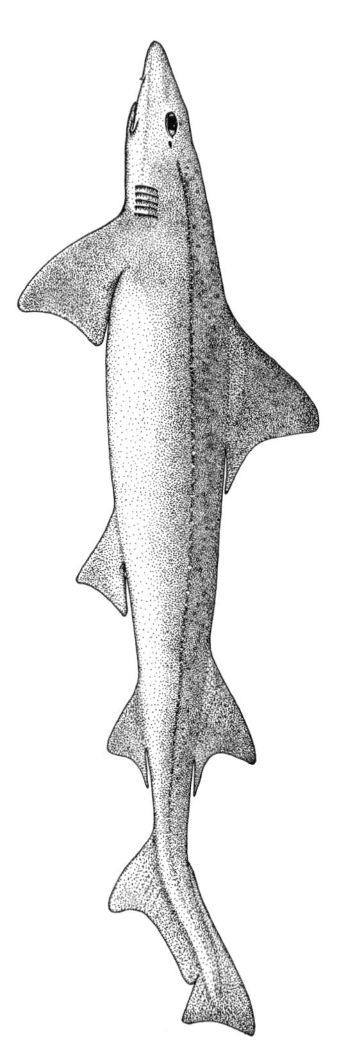

KAPETĀ, MANGĀ, MANGŌ, PIOKE
RIG

Mustelus lenticulatus

Description: Mid-grey with an off-white belly and numerous white spots over the upper body, this shark has an elongated shape with a short, pointed snout. The head is slightly flattened, with oval eyes and a broad mouth armed with small, flat teeth laid out like paving. The two dorsal fins are broad and bluntly pointed; the first is large and sail-like, positioned between the pectoral and pelvic fins, and the second is smaller and slightly ahead of the anal fin. The tail is small, the upper lobe larger than the lower, with a D-shaped notch. Females grow to just over 1.5m in total length, the slightly smaller males to just over 1.1m.

Distribution in Aotearoa: Endemic. Rigs occur around mainland Aotearoa and Rēkohu Wharekauri Chatham Islands.

Habitat: Benthic, found on sand and muddy bottoms from the subtidal to 250m depth. They are uncommon at the deeper end of this range.

Curator's notes: This shark is considered good to eat and there is a commercial fishery as well as recreational catch; it is often marketed as 'lemonfish'. Although superficially similar to spiny dogfish (*Squalus acanthias*, page 23) rigs lack dorsal spines and have an anal fin. Their teeth are not used for cutting but for crushing hard-bodied invertebrates such as crabs and molluscs; they will also take soft-bodied prey such as worms. Females pup in harbours and estuaries, producing up to 24 young, so degradation of these habitats is of concern.

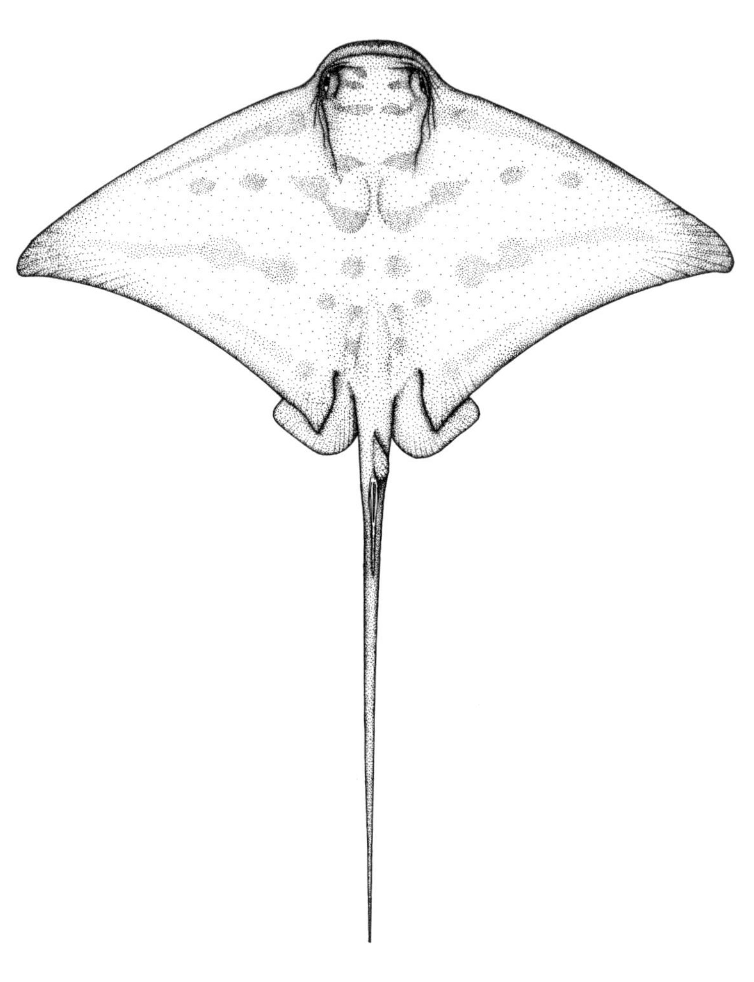

WHAI REPO
EAGLE RAY

Myliobatis tenuicaudatus

Description: This ray has a dark olive-grey upper body with bright blue blotches and lines and is white underneath. The elongated, pointed wings are slightly swept back. A humped head protrudes beyond the front of the wings. The eyes have a large spiracle behind each, and the mouth underneath the body is broad with flattened teeth laid out like paving. The pelvic fins are prominent just before the tail. The dorsal fin is small, positioned behind the pelvic fins. The tail is rounded and whip-like, armed with one to three strong, serrated venomous spines. The whai repo can grow to a little over 1m across the body.

Distribution in Aotearoa: Found around the mainland, more commonly around Te Ika-a-Māui North Island.

Habitat: Most often seen in harbours, estuaries and sandy beaches, uncommon below 50m depth.

Curator's notes: Swimmers and those using seine nets at the beach have trodden on this ray and suffered excruciatingly painful stab wounds from tail spines as the ray lashes out in panic. These are, in fact, gentle and curious fishes that will cautiously approach swimmers and divers. People should employ the 'stingray shuffle' in cloudy shallow water by sliding their feet through the sand to warn the ray of their approach and give it time to escape. Eagle rays prey on invertebrates often buried in the sand. These are uncovered when the ray squirts a strong stream of water from its mouth, leaving characteristic shallow pits in the sand. Its flattened teeth are for crushing.

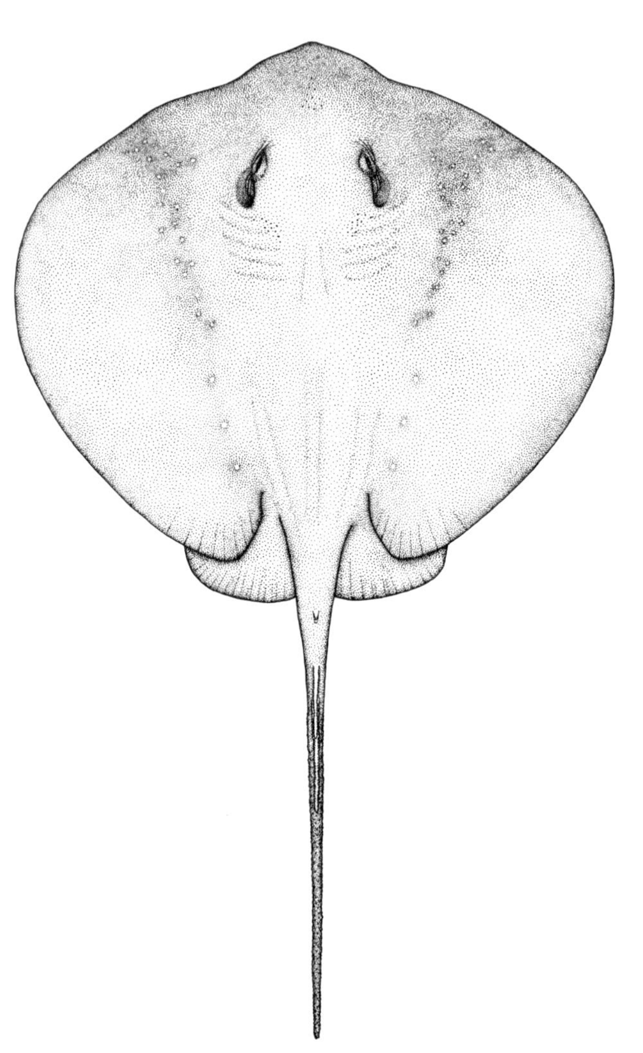

ORU, PĀKAU, PĀKAURUA, ROHA, WHAI, WHAI REPO
SHORTTAIL STINGRAY

Bathytoshia brevicaudata

Description: This ray is dark grey to blue grey on the upper body with a line of white spots behind the eyes. Its body is a diamond shape and thicker along the centreline. It has large eyes and a mouth armed with rows of small pointed teeth curved slightly back. The short, rounded and tapering tail is armed with one to three large serrated spines with venomous tissue. This species is among the largest and heaviest marine stingrays, growing to over 2m in width across the body and 350kg in weight.

Distribution in Aotearoa: Very widespread, occurring from Rangitāhua Kermadec Islands to Rakiura Stewart Island and Rēkohu Wharekauri Chatham Islands.

Habitat: Often encountered in harbours and estuaries, and also found on sandy beaches and reefs. These strong swimmers are capable of traversing across wide expanses of open ocean.

Curator's notes: Frequently seen with eagle rays (*Myliobatis tenuicaudatus*, page 27), swimmers in murky shallow water should use the same shuffle-walking technique to avoid injury. A very curious fish, they will frequently approach divers; while the author was diving, a small one kept positioning itself over his head to be massaged by exhaled bubbles. Some have become extremely tame and can be hand-fed. If they feel threatened, they will raise their tail as a warning. Large rays are capable of inflicting fatal wounds with their spines. Prey is commonly crabs and molluscs, which are often buried in the sediment. Like eagle rays, stingrays will blow a stream of water down to expose their prey and leave a patchwork of characteristic depressions in the sea bed.

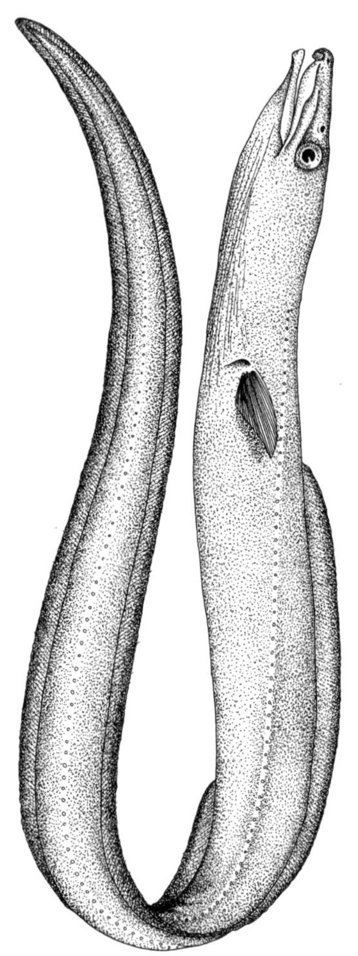

KOIERO, KŌIRO, KŌRIRO, NGŌIRO, NGOINGOI, NGOIO, NGŌIRO, TOTOKE

CONGER EEL

Conger verreauxi

Description: This eel is dark brown to dark blue-grey, but paler around the lower jaw and belly. Its body is flattened towards the tail. It has a large head and mouth with thick lips, extending back to below about mid-eye. The teeth are small and in two rows, the outer row compressed and peg-shaped, forming a cutting edge. The dorsal fin begins approximately over the tip of the well-developed pectoral fins. The conger eel grows to at least 2m total length.

Distribution in Aotearoa: Widespread around the coast from Rangitāhua Kermadec Islands to Tini Heke Snares Islands, and east to Rēkohu Wharekauri Chatham Islands, from 0 to usually 200m depth, but occasionally to nearly 600m depth.

Habitat: During the day, often found hidden in crevices in reefs, or in rubbish and objects such as pipes.

Curator's notes: This is one of two coastal species of conger eel, the other being smaller and more northern in distribution. The conger eel's eyesight is rather poor, and they can react aggressively if they feel threatened by divers. Most active at night, they hunt for smaller invertebrates and fishes. Some may closely follow divers moving through stands of kelp to pick up any crabs or other animals that get disturbed. When conger eels become sexually mature, the body becomes gelatinous, the eyes get larger, the internal organs degenerate and the cavity becomes packed with testes or ovaries. This readies them to spawn once, and then they die.

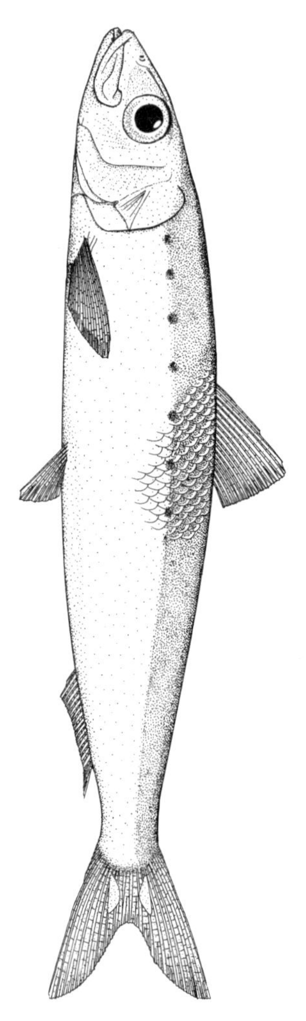

MOHIMOHI
PILCHARD

Sardinops sagax

Description: The mohimohi is silvery with a bright blue to blue-green sheen over the back, a silvery white belly and 8 to 14 black spots along the mid-flank. Its body is shallow, compressed and elongate with moderately small scales that shed easily when the fish is caught. The mouth extends back to below the front of its large eyes. The dorsal fin is positioned about mid-body and the caudal fin is forked. The pectoral fins are set near the lower edge of the body. This fish has many long gill rakers. It can grow up to 22.5cm standard length.

Distribution in Aotearoa: Coastal waters around the country.

Habitat: Although oceanic, most likely seen in harbours and sheltered waters.

Curator's notes: Mohimohi can form vast schools, sometimes measuring kilometres in length, and are vitally important as food for seabirds, marine mammals and larger fishes. Large schools can fall victim to mass mortality from a herpes-type virus, which attacks the gills. There is a small commercial and recreational catch around Aotearoa, though they are almost always either used as bait or fed to pets, and are overlooked as a good fish to eat. Overfishing has seen the sizes of schools diminish around Aotearoa; rapid growth and breeding would see this quickly reversed if it were stopped. Originally up to five species were recognised, but these are now considered to be local populations of just one global species. They feed on plankton, which they sieve out of the water using their long gill rakers.

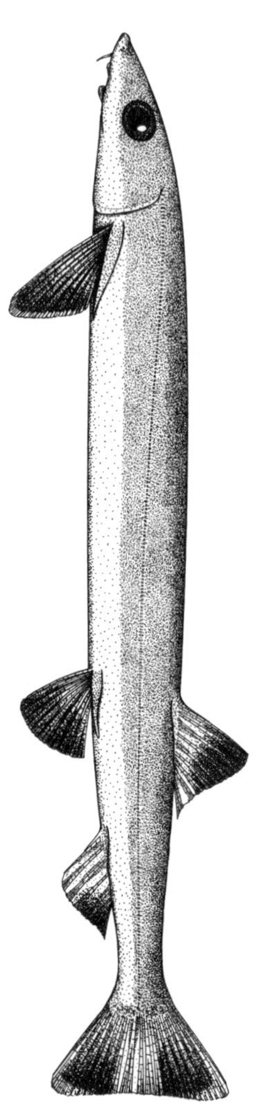

SANDFISH

Gonorynchus forsteri

Description: This fish is light brown on the upper head and body, grading to orange red on the lower flanks and belly. The fins have a species-specific pattern of black and white. Its body is elongate and cylindrical, and entirely covered with small scales that are rough to the touch. The snout is pointed, with a small mouth underneath, ahead of the eyes, with a small barbel just ahead of the mouth. The eyes are large and round. The dorsal fin is triangular and positioned over the pelvic fins, towards the rear of the body. The tail is fan-shaped. The pectoral fins are positioned low on the body. Sandfish grow to over 55cm standard length.

Distribution in Aotearoa: Widespread around the coast.

Habitat: Found on clean sandy bottoms where they bury themselves during the day, emerging at night to feed. They have been caught by trawlers at depths of up to 1200m.

Curator's notes: This species' need for clean sand means that it is now absent from many of our larger harbours. Rarely caught by anglers, these attractive fish are often encountered by divers at night, when they can be seen foraging in the sand for food (sand hoppers, sea lice, worms, brittle stars and small fishes). When disturbed, they will bury themselves quickly; at this point a plastic bag can be placed over the location and the fish caught. Another common name, 'sand eel', reflects this behaviour, and 'beaked salmon' references the colour of their flesh. A second, rarer, tropical species, Gray's sandfish, is found around Te Ika-a-Māui North Island. These fishes appear to spawn like eels, becoming soft-bodied, migrating along the Norfolk Ridge and dying shortly afterwards.

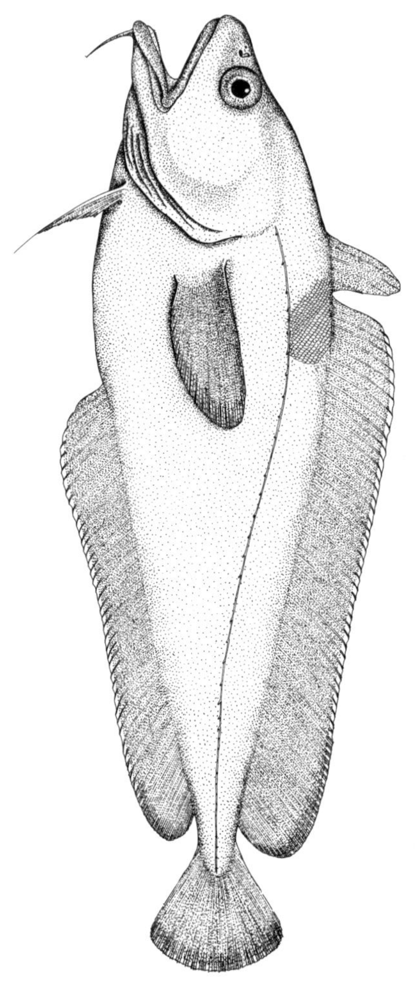

ROCK COD

Lotella rhacina

Description: The rock cod varies from brick red to deep chocolate brown, and pinkish to off-white in the belly region. It has an elongated body, with a short, rounded head. It is rounded through the abdomen, which increasingly compresses and tapers towards the tail. The large mouth extends back beyond the eyes and is armed with several rows of small canine teeth. The chin has a small, stout barbel. The first dorsal fin is short and erect; the second is long, extending almost to the upper base of the tail. The caudal fin is lobate. The large pectoral fins are positioned at mid-body. The small pelvic fins are positioned on the lower belly and have a long outer ray. The long anal fin has a slight indentation in the middle and is positioned approximately opposite the second dorsal fin. This is the largest species in the genus, growing to over 34cm standard length.

Distribution in Aotearoa: Widespread from Rangitāhua Kermadec Islands to Rakiura Stewart Island and Rēkohu Wharekauri Chatham Islands.

Habitat: Found on coastal reefs down to 30m depth. It sits in holes and caves during the day, emerging at dusk to forage for food.

Curator's notes: A graceful and attractive species, once acclimatised the rock cod does well in an aquarium and can be trained to be hand-fed. Rock cod feed by explosively opening their mouths and sucking items in. The barbel is sensitive to chemical traces and vibrations from prey, and is held out away from the mouth so it can hunt in darkness. Rock cod can host a wide range of interesting parasites.

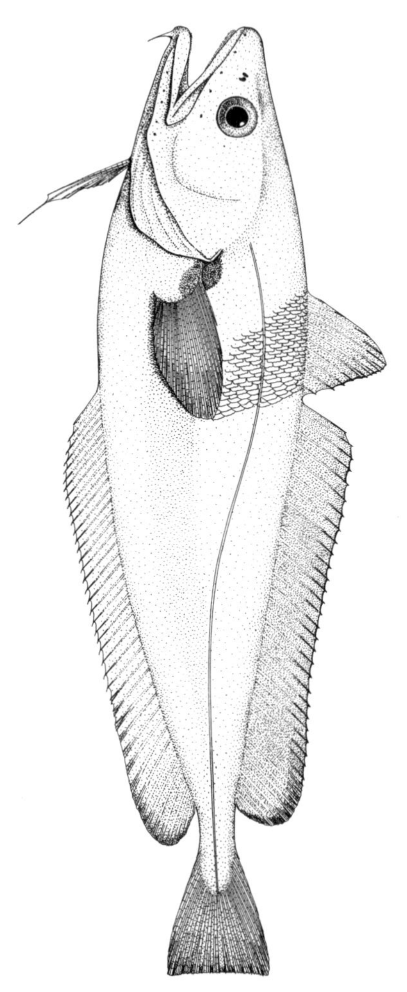

HOKA
RED COD

Pseudophycis bachus

Description: The hoka varies from from brick-red to pinkish brown, darker above and grading to off-white and pink from the chin across the belly and above the anal fin. A distinctive dark brown-black blotch on the body above the pectoral fins extends onto the base of the upper fin rays. It has a broad, cavernous head. A large mouth extends beyond the back of the large round eyes, armed with broad bands of tiny teeth. The chin has a small barbel. The caudal fin has a squared-off end. Large pectoral fins are positioned at mid-body. Small pelvic fins with a long outer ray are positioned on the lower belly. The anal fin lies approximately opposite, and is as long as, the second dorsal fin. This species is the biggest in the genus, growing to 65cm standard length.

Distribution in Aotearoa: An endemic species, found around the coast from Otou North Cape to Motu Ihupuku Campbell Islands, east to Rēkohu Wharekauri Chatham and south to Moutere Hauriri Bounty Islands.

Habitat: Found on muddy to sandy bottoms and on coastal reefs, from the subtidal to 570m depth.

Curator's notes: Originally thought to occur on both sides of Te Tai-o-Rehua Tasman Sea, recent research has found the Australian species to be different. Like others in the morid cod family, they are more active at night. Prey consists of crabs and other fishes; like the rock cod (*Lotella rhacina*, page 37), the barbel is used to detect prey in the dark. Often forming large schools, red cod are targeted commercially and recreationally, but they are not popular because their flesh is soft. This can be improved by leaving it to sit in the fridge.

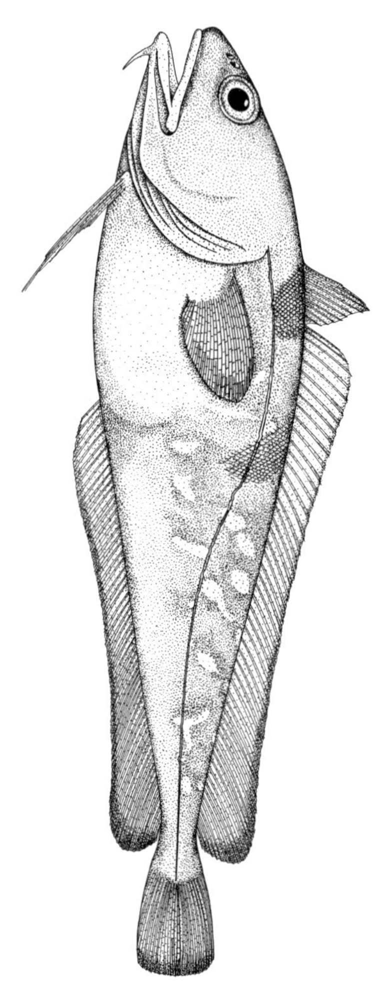

SOUTHERN BASTARD COD

Pseudophycis barbata

Description: The southern bastard cod is brick red to dark brown, darker above and often with irregular pale blotches across the flanks. It has a broad, cavernous head. A large mouth extends beyond the back of the large, round eyes and is armed with broad bands of tiny teeth. The chin has a small barbel. The caudal fin has a rounded end. Large pectoral fins are positioned at mid-body. The small pelvic fins are positioned on the lower belly and have a long outer ray. The anal fin is positioned approximately opposite, and is as long as, the second dorsal fin. It grows to 62cm standard length.

Distribution in Aotearoa: Around the coast from Manawatāwhi Three Kings Islands to the southern Snares Shelf, and east to Rēkohu Wharekauri Chatham Islands.

Habitat: Most common on coastal reefs in 0 to 520m depth.

Curator's notes: Unlike red cod (*Pseudophycis bachus*, page 39), this species is solitary. As with others in the morid cod family, they are more active at night. Prey consists of crabs and other fishes. The uncouth common name is a corruption of *barbata*, which means 'having a beard', in reference to the barbel. The pale blotches on the body give rise to another common name, cloudy bay cod. There is an incidental commercial catch as well as an occasional recreational one. A third smaller species, the northern bastard cod (*Pseudophycis breviuscula*), is found around Te Ika-a-Māui North Island and is distinguished by having larger scales.

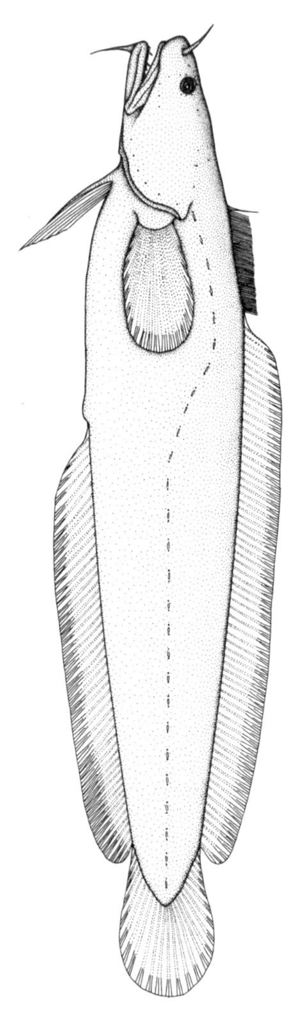

ROCKLING

Gaidropsarus novaezealandiae

Description: The rockling is a uniform red brown to dark chocolate-brown colour. It has a slender, elongated body, rounded anteriorly, becoming compressed towards the tail. The head is small with a wide mouth that extends beyond the back of the small, round eyes. Its jaws are armed with small but distinct fangs. The chin has a large barbel supplemented by two more off the snout, by the nostrils. The first dorsal fin is a single isolated ray over the pectoral fin base, followed by a short tuft of fleshy filaments. The pectoral fins are large and rounded whereas the pelvic fins are slender and narrow, set below the gill opening with an elongate outer ray. The anal fin is the same shape as the second dorsal fin but shorter. The caudal fin is lobate. Rockling grow to 30cm standard length.

Distribution in Aotearoa: Around the coast from Te Tairāwhiti East Cape to the southern Tini Heke Snares Islands.

Habitat: On reefs and in rockpools, holes and caves. Commonly encountered down to 50m depth, but some specimens have been found at depths of up to 500m, where they are less likely to be caught.

Curator's notes: Rockling are solitary and secretive. When observed by divers using a torch, they swim rapidly in circles before wriggling into a crack. Larvae of this species are found right across the southern hemisphere, but despite this, and an abundance of suitable habitats, none have yet been collected from Rēkohu Wharekauri Chatham Islands. Very large numbers occur at Ōkahu Jackson Bay, which coincides with where the trans-Tasman Current reaches the coast of Aotearoa. Warming sea temperatures mean that this species has been seen less frequently in its northern limits.

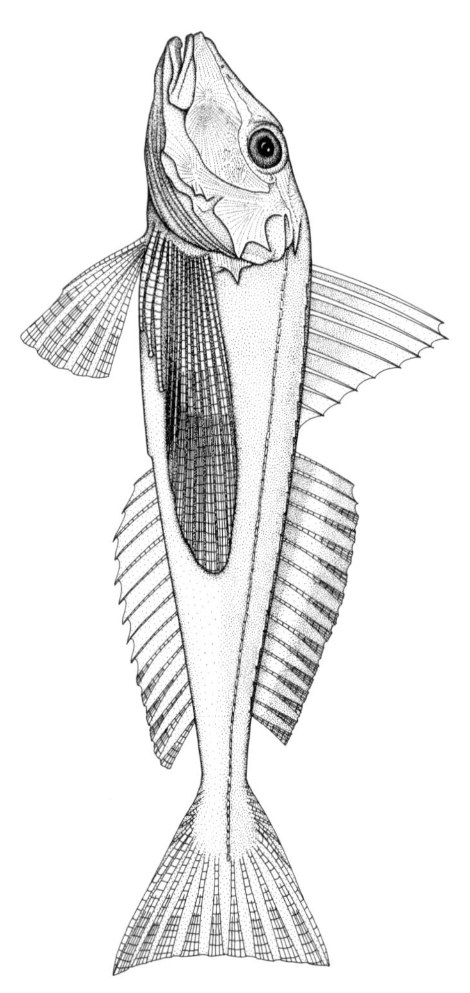

KUMUKUMU, PŪWHAIAU
RED GURNARD

Chelidonichthys kumu

Description: This fish is bright red on top with irregular darker blotches, and pearl white underneath including the anal fin. The pectoral fins are a brilliant green with electric-blue spots and margin, and a large black eyespot on the inner face. Its body tapers towards the tail. The head is heavily armoured, triangular and flattened underneath. The mouth extends beyond the front of the round eyes, which are high on the head. The first dorsal fin consists of slender spines; the second dorsal fin of soft rays. The caudal fin is emarginate. The pectoral fins are very large; the lower has separate thickened rays. The pelvic fins are positioned directly under the pectoral fins. The anal fin mirrors the second dorsal fin. Red gurnard grow to 50cm standard length.

Distribution in Aotearoa: Widespread around both main islands and Rēhoku Wharekauri Chatham Islands.

Habitat: Found on sandy to muddy sea beds, especially where there is lace coral and shell hash, which supports an abundance of prey.

Curator's notes: These fish are often seen 'walking' over the sea bed on their thickened lower pectoral fin rays. The rays have joints that enable them to bend forward like a hand and are also extremely sensitive to any movement by animals living in the sand. When movement is detected, the red gurnard lunges and grabs. Prey includes worms, crustaceans and small fishes. Muscles attached to the swim bladder are used to create a very loud drumming and croaking sound. At night they are much paler, making the blotches stand out. A valuable commercial and prized recreational species.

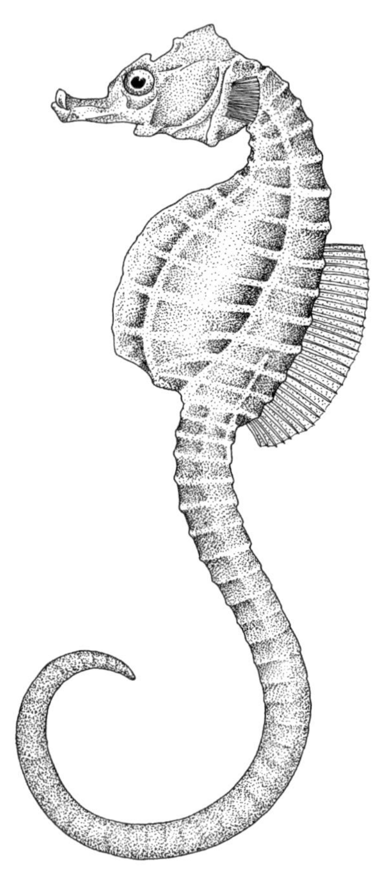

HINAMOKI, KIORE MOANA, KIORE WAITAI, MANAIA

SEAHORSE

Hippocampus abdominalis

Description: This seahorse is pale tan to golden brown with darker irregular spots and blotches. The head and body appear as bony plates covered with skin. A single dorsal fin is positioned about mid-body. The pectoral fins are small and fan-shaped. A minute anal fin of four to five rays is positioned immediately below the anus. There are variable numbers of filamentous tassels on the head and upper body of males, which also have a bulbous, smooth belly for brooding eggs. *Hippocampus abdominalis* is the largest species of seahorse in the world, growing to 21cm total length with some evidence of even larger ones.

Distribution in Aotearoa: An endemic species, found around Aotearoa including Rēkohu Wharekauri Chatham Islands. The IUCN lists them as Least Concern, although harvesting for traditional Asian medicine has seen them locally depleted from several areas around Aotearoa. Loss of large kelp beds in harbours because of pollution and sedimentation also reduces their numbers.

Habitat: Found in sheltered bays and harbours in association with large brown algae, especially giant kelp.

Curator's notes: Feeding mainly on small crustaceans, seahorses have a strike as quick as 3 milliseconds. Larger shrimps are broken up by repeated strikes until small enough to swallow. Seahorses will only feed on live prey, making them challenging to keep in aquaria. Females deposit their eggs in the brood pouches of a number of males in the immediate area; depending on the size of the male they can carry from 40 to over 300 eggs, which take about a month to develop and are expelled at night. The species is vulnerable to collecting as they rely on camouflage and 'freezing' for protection rather than rapidly swimming away. They swim by undulating their dorsal fin while holding their body straight, and they manoeuvre by rapidly fluttering their small pectoral fins.

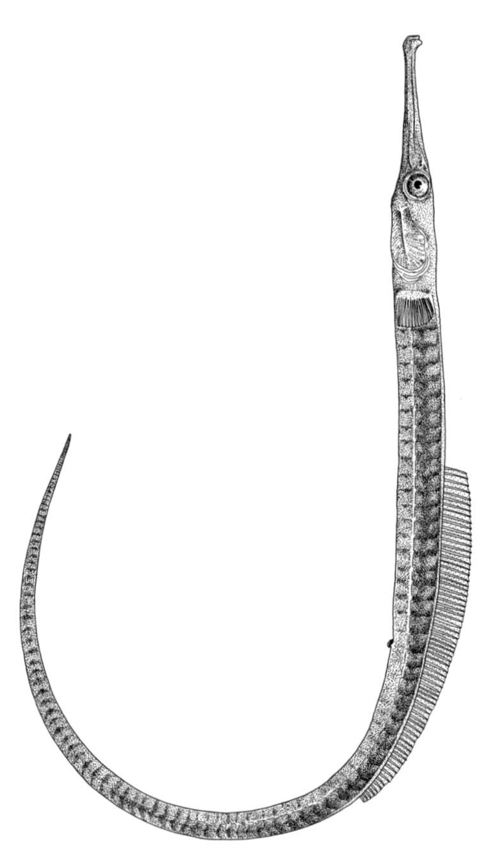

SMOOTH PIPEFISH

Stigmatophora macropterygia

Description: The smooth pipefish is brown to golden tan with fine speckling over the head; some specimens have paired dark spots along the upper body. The long snout is about 62–73 percent of the head length and is turned up at the mouth. Its body is a series of bony rings covered with skin. The long dorsal fin has 63 to 74 fin rays. The pectoral fins are fan-shaped. There are no anal or caudal fins. Males carry the eggs in a bulbous fleshy fold on the belly about mid-body; females often have an elongate, fleshy hood-like lateral fold. Maximum size is 40cm total length.

Distribution in Aotearoa: An endemic species, widespread around Aotearoa from Te Tai Tokerau Northland to Motu Maha Auckland Islands. It is more common in southern regions, and along the east coast, especially in sheltered areas. The introduced *Undaria* seaweed has displaced many of the native kelp species that previously hosted this pipefish and has led to a decline in their numbers, especially in sheltered waters. The IUCN lists this species as Least Concern, but, as noted, their preferred algae have been displaced so they are seen less often.

Habitat: Associated with stands of large brown native kelp species in depths of 0 to 20m, usually less than 10m.

Curator's notes: Smooth pipefish are not fast swimmers and rely on looking like a displaced piece of kelp stem to avoid potential predators. They usually swim with their bodies rigid, undulating the long dorsal fin to move forward or backwards. The long tail is slightly prehensile, capable of anchoring them in rough conditions. They feed on the small crustaceans and tiny fishes that live among the seaweed. Like seahorses (*Hippocampus abdominalis*, page 47), they will only take live food.

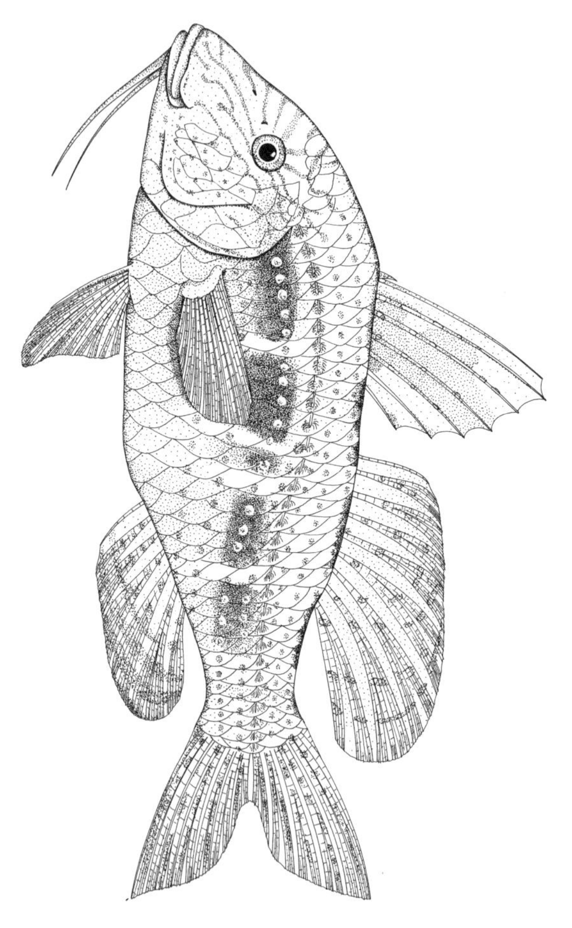

AHURUHURU
GOATFISH, RED MULLET

Upenichthys porosus

Description: The ahuruhuru has a highly variable colour. Mature males are especially colourful, with broken blue lines that cross the head and lines of blue-green dots running along the flanks, becoming blue-violet further down the flank and radiating out across the tail. Smaller specimens, and females, tend to be red over the head and body with irregular black to brown blotches along the mid-flank; when feeding over sand, the colour fades. Its body is short and oval, with a humped back profile and a flattened belly. The mouth is on the underside with two long fleshy barbels off the tip of the lower jaw. The round eyes are high on the head. The first dorsal fin has one short and seven long, slender spines. The caudal fin is deeply forked. The pectoral fins are fan-shaped, with the pelvic fins directly underneath. The anal fin is opposite the second dorsal fin. Maximum size is 36cm standard length.

Distribution in Aotearoa: An endemic species, found from Rangitāhua Kermadec Islands and around Te Ika-a-Māui North Island, straggling to the outer Te Tauihu-o-te-waka Marlborough Sounds.

Habitat: Found on reefs and sand around coastal areas in 0 to 70m depth.

Curator's notes: Females often school whereas males tend to be larger and more solitary. Barbels are flicked across the sea bed, 'tasting' for prey, such as worms, crustaceans and small fishes. Often prey is scooped up with a mouthful of sand, which has to be expelled out of the gills. There is a small commercial and recreational catch. The name 'red mullet' refers to the firm texture and oily flavour of the flesh, which resembles mullet.

RED-BANDED PERCH

Hypoplectrodes huntii

Description: This fish has a tan body and a brownish tan head crossed with orange-red bands. The body is crossed with seven wide, dark reddish-brown bands. The fins are red to orange and the belly off-white. Its body is short, oval and compressed. The head is large with a sizeable mouth that extends to below about mid-eye. It has large, round eyes on the upper head. The dorsal fin has 10 strong sharp spines. The caudal fin is large and fan-shaped. The pectoral fins are in a fan shape and the pelvic fins lie under the base of the pectorals. The anal fin spines are very large and strong. Maximum size is 20cm standard length.

Distribution in Aotearoa: An endemic species, widespread around Aotearoa, from Manawatāwhi Three Kings Islands to the southern Tini Heke Shelf, and east to Rēkohu Wharekauri Chatham Islands. Four similar species are known from around Aotearoa, of which the eyebrow perch (*Hypoplectrodes* sp. A) reaches 47cm standard length.

Habitat: Found on reefs with abundant holes and caves, in 2 to 70m depth.

Curator's notes: A solitary species, red-banded perches are most often seen resting in holes and caves by divers looking for spiny lobsters. Very occasionally they are caught by recreational anglers. They are eclectic predators, generally targeting crabs and other smaller fishes. They make colourful aquarium inhabitants but need a large tank with plenty of hiding places along with high-quality water, and they will usually eat their smaller tankmates.

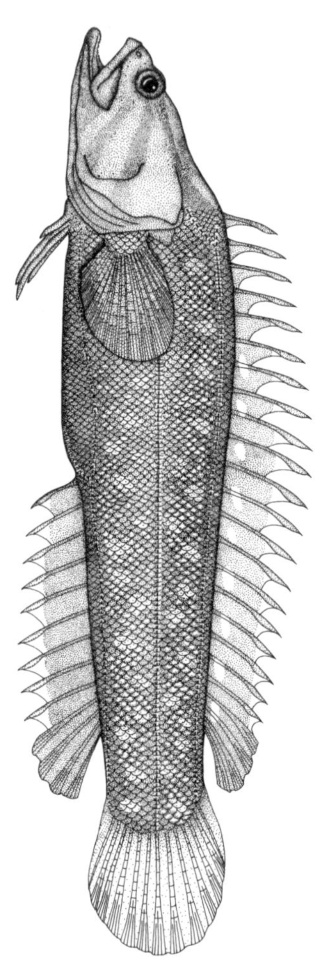

TAUMAKA
OLIVE ROCKFISH

Acanthoclinus fuscus

Description: Olive green to grey with off-white mottling, the taumaka has a white blaze across the head from the start of the dorsal fin to the snout, and dark lines radiate from the eyes across the head. Its body is very elongate, slender and oval, becoming compressed towards the tail. The moderately sized head has a large mouth that extends to below about mid-eye. It has large, round eyes on the upper head. The dorsal fin runs for most of the length of the body with 20 sharp spines and four soft rays. The caudal fin is lobe-shaped. The pectoral fins are large and fan-shaped and the pelvic fins long and slender, positioned under the gill opening. The anal fin is similar to the dorsal but shorter. The taumaka has three lateral lines along the body, the lowest splitting into two across the belly. Maximum size is 22.8cm standard length.

Distribution in Aotearoa: An endemic species, widespread around the mainland coast but absent from off-shore islands.

Habitat: On reefs and rocky shores and in estuaries, in 0 to 10m depth.

Curator's notes: This species shows extreme tolerance to a wide range of water quality and salinity: they have been found at low tide under rocks where fresh water flows, while at high tide they are fully marine. They are commonly encountered at low tide under exposed rocks. Males find and defend a nest site under a suitable rock. The female is driven off after laying her eggs and the male blocks the entrance. Once the young hatch, the entrance is unblocked and they swim a short distance away before settling onto the seabed. The olive rockfish is excellent for marine aquaria as it quickly adapts to captivity, is not fussy about food and can live for up to nine years.

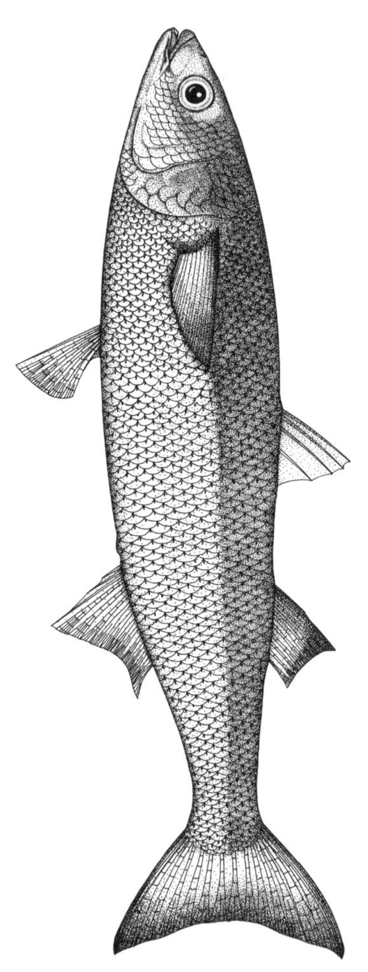

AUA, AWA, KĀTAHA, KATAKA MAKAWHITI, MARAHEA, MARAUA, MATAKĀ, MATAKAWHITI, MOKOWHITI, PŌNAHO

YELLOWEYE MULLET

Aldrichetta forsteri

Description: The yelloweye mullet has a silver head and a body that is blue to blue green above and bright white below. It has bright yellow irises and a yellow streak along the flank. The large, round body is moderately elongate and slender. It has a pointed snout with a small mouth and very large eyes set mid-head. The first dorsal fin comprises slender, elongate spines and the second has one spine and nine to ten soft rays. The caudal fin is large and forked. The pectoral fins are small and angular. The pelvic fins are positioned directly under the pectoral fins. The anal fin is opposite, and the same size as, the second dorsal fin. Maximum size is 36cm standard length.

Distribution in Aotearoa: Widespread around the coast of the main islands, and east to Rēkohu Wharekauri Chatham Islands.

Habitat: Estuaries (occasionally up rivers) and coastal regions, from 0 to 50m depth.

Curator's notes: Sometimes incorrectly called 'herring', this species is frequently the first fish caught by young anglers. They form large schools that move in and out of estuaries and the lower reaches of rivers, and along the coast. Fish usually school by same-size classes. Juveniles tend to shelter in estuaries for periods of time. Their prey is invertebrates, especially crustaceans, and detritus consumed off the mud. In turn, these fish are eaten by seabirds and larger fish such as kahawai (*Arripis trutta*, page 69). Although bony, these fish are considered good to eat.

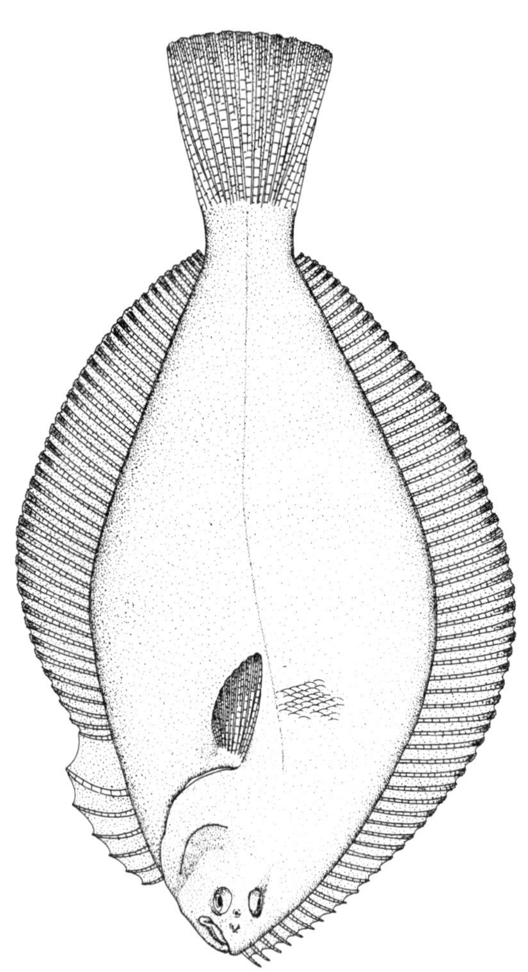

PĀTIKI TŌTARA, PĀTŌTARA, RATUTU, WHAIWHAI

YELLOWBELLY FLOUNDER

Rhombosolea leporina

Description: The yellowbelly flounder is dark grey to olive green on its right (ocular) side, with occasional tiny black spots; the underside (blind side) is yellowish white. It has an oval body shape. The snout protrudes slightly with a very small fleshy lobe. All fins comprise only soft rays. The caudal fin is emarginate. Maximum size is 45cm standard length.

Distribution in Aotearoa: An endemic species, widespread around the coast, also at Rēkohu Wharekauri Chatham Islands. Although not listed by the IUCN, the related sand flounder is recorded as having a decreasing population trend. Given that the preferred habitat of the yellowbelly flounder is becoming more degraded, this species could also be at risk.

Habitat: Sheltered harbours and estuaries on clean sand and mud, in 0 to 30m depth. They do not venture into pure fresh water.

Curator's notes: One of the 'right-eyed' flounders. To determine this, hold the flounder with the tail towards you and the head away, and the anus pointed down; then see which side the eyes are on. Right-eyed flounders are better for eating than left-eyed species found around Aotearoa; left-eyed species are in a different family, Bothidae. Four species of flounder are known in the genus *Rhombosolea*, and all are good to eat, but the yellowbelly is considered to be the best. Their prey are small invertebrates that live in and on the sea bed. They swim by undulating the dorsal and anal fins with the pectoral fin on the eye side held up like a rudder. Fast swimming is achieved by rippling the whole body.

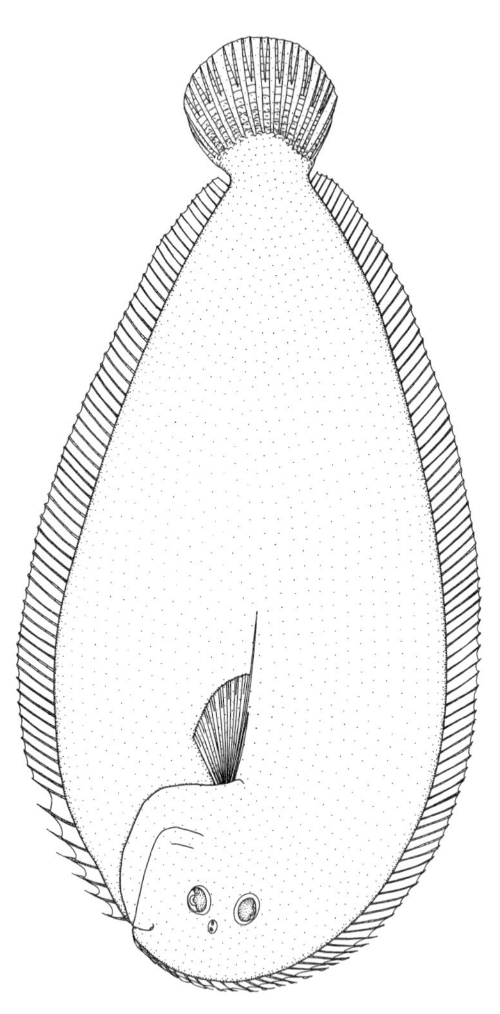

KUTUHORI, PAKEKE, PĀTIKI RORE, PĀTIKI RORI, RAUTUTU, TARORE
COMMON SOLE

Peltorhamphus novaezeelandiae

Description: The common sole is greenish to grey brown with a few scattered large darker blotches on the right (ocular) side. The blind side is off-white. Like all flatfishes, it can adjust its colour and increase speckling to match its background. The head and body are teardrop-shaped and depressed; the head is rounded with a fleshy hook obscuring the mouth. The dorsal and anal fins follow the body margin almost to the lobe-shaped caudal fin, and the anterior rays are much shorter than those mid-body. The pectoral fin is a slender lobe with one ray, closest to the eyes, being extremely long. Maximum size is 52.5cm standard length.

Distribution in Aotearoa: An endemic species found around the coast, less commonly along the west coast of Te Waipounamu South Island.

Habitat: Sandy bays, harbours and estuaries on clean sand, in 0 to 55m depth. Its range can extend into deeper water.

Curator's notes: This is a very common species of flounder, most often seen by divers at night. There are four species in the genus, which are all endemic. The other three are small, not exceeding 16cm standard length. The common sole feeds on shrimps and other benthic invertebrates. Tiny fleshy outgrowths around the lower jaw are used to detect prey. Juvenile soles are targeted by skates, red cod and other larger fishes. Swimming is the same as for the yellowbelly flounder (*Rhombosolea leporina*, page 59). The common sole is the most abundant commercially caught flounder species in New Zealand waters.

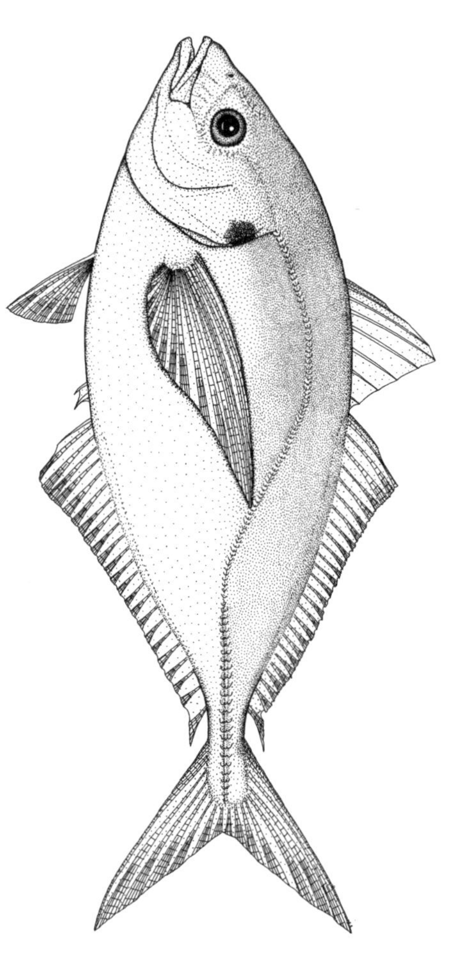

ARARA, ARĀRA, KOMUTUMUTU, KOPAPA, RAUMARIE, RAUMARIE ĀRĀRA, RUAMARIE, RUAMARIE ĀRĀRA

TREVALLY

Pseudocaranx georgianus

Description: The trevally is silvery with a blue to blue-green hue over the back with violet flashes, a brilliant white lower surface and a yellow or grey tail. It has a rounded and compressed head and body. The mouth extends to the front edges of the eyes and has small, conical teeth and thick lips, especially on adults. The first dorsal fin has long slender spines; the second a single spine and 25 to 29 soft rays, with the last ray almost detached from the rest of the fin. The large caudal fin is deeply forked. The pectoral fins are long and falcate, with the pelvic fins positioned underneath. The anal fin has two strong spines unconnected to the rest of the fin, which has soft rays about equal in length to the second dorsal fin. It has large, armoured lateral-line scales at the rear, forming a keel (sharp edge) just before the tail. Older fish develop a marked hump over the head. Maximum size is 82.7cm fork length.

Distribution in Aotearoa: Widespread, found from Rangitāhua Kermadec Islands to Rakiura Stewart Island and east to Rēkohu Wharekauri Chatham Islands, in 0 to 240m depth. They are more abundant in northern waters.

Habitat: A schooling pelagic species that moves widely from estuaries to the open ocean.

Curator's notes: A popular game fish, trevally can form large schools of big fish at the surface, especially if schooling crustaceans like *Munida* are present in sizeable numbers. Initial growth is rapid but slows after about 30cm. The skeletons of trevally have some excessively thickened bones, called Tilly bones after the nickname of the scientist, Johanna Edinger, who described them. In trevally, these are the bony crest over the head and one of the spines on the backbone. Bigger fish that feed on the bottom often have well-developed papillae around the mouth.

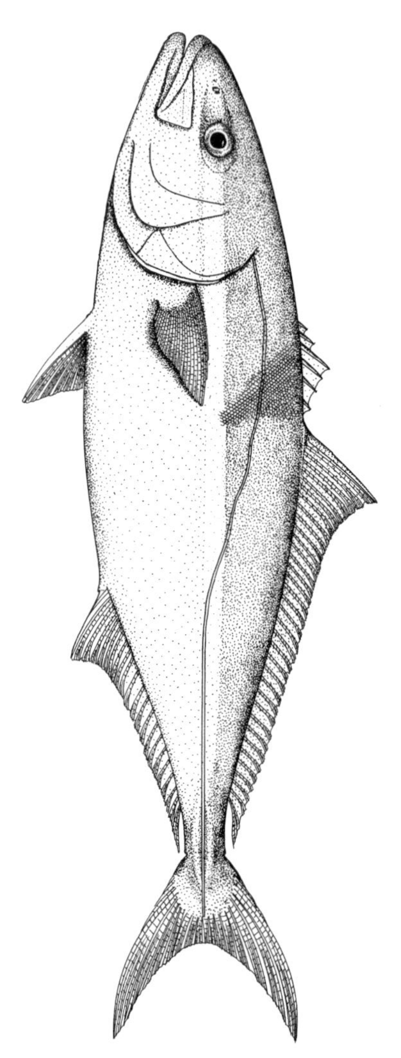

HAKU, KAHU, MAKUMAKU, WAREHENGA

KINGFISH

Seriola lalandi

Description: The kingfish is iridescent blue to blue green over the back with a strong yellow stripe across the head, through the eyes and to the base of the tail. Below the stripe the fish is off-white. It has a streamlined body with the head and body fusiform and muscular. The mouth has minute teeth in bands on both jaws, which extend back to under the rounded eyes. The first dorsal fin is very low with moderately strong spines. The caudal fin is deeply forked. The pectoral fins are small and slightly pointed; the pelvic fins are about same size and under the pectoral fins. The anal fin has two isolated small, strong spines, and soft rays mirroring the shape of the second dorsal fin. The lateral line scales at the rear are not enlarged to form scutes. Maximum size is 1.93m total length.

Distribution in Aotearoa: Wide-ranging, from Rangitāhua Kermadec Islands to off Ōtepoti Dunedin, occurring more commonly in southern regions during summer.

Habitat: Moves freely from harbours and estuaries to the open ocean, following prey.

Curator's notes: Kingfish are a highly prized gamefish. They frequently associate with flotsam such as logs. A curious species, they will also approach divers. These fish are voracious hunters of smaller fishes. Three other species in the genus *Seriola* have been recorded from Aotearoa (amberjack, almaco jack and samsonfish), but these are stragglers and are rarely seen. However, increasing sea temperatures may see them become more common. Fishes in east Australia often have a parasite that turns the flesh soft and milky when cooked.

GIANT BOARFISH

Partistiopterus labiosus

Description: The colour of this fish varies, but it is usually silvery with dark brown on the head and two irregular oblique bars across the body. Mature males are believed to be darker with a myriad of yellow spots and blotches. Its head and body are oval and compressed; the snout and body become longer with age. The short mouth does not extend as far as the front edges of the eyes. The profile of the upper head rises steeply up to the dorsal fin, which has seven long, strong spines followed by 16–18 soft rays. The tail is squared to emarginate. The pectoral fins are slightly falcate. The short anal fin is positioned under the back end of the dorsal fin. Maximum size is 90cm standard length.

Distribution in Aotearoa: From Rangitāhua Kermadec Islands to around Aotearoa. It is less common around Te Waipounamu South Island, where it straggles to Ōtepoti Dunedin.

Habitat: Seen in small to large schools on deeper reefs and sandy areas in 10 to 170m depth.

Curator's notes: The common name comes from their observed behaviour of rooting around in sand to catch prey (crabs, worms, fishes, etc.). A long-lived fish, numbers have been depleted in shallower waters by the recreational catch, but, with growing awareness, spearfishers have been taking fewer and recovery has been seen in some areas. Anglers are urged to return this species to the water alive to assist in their recovery.

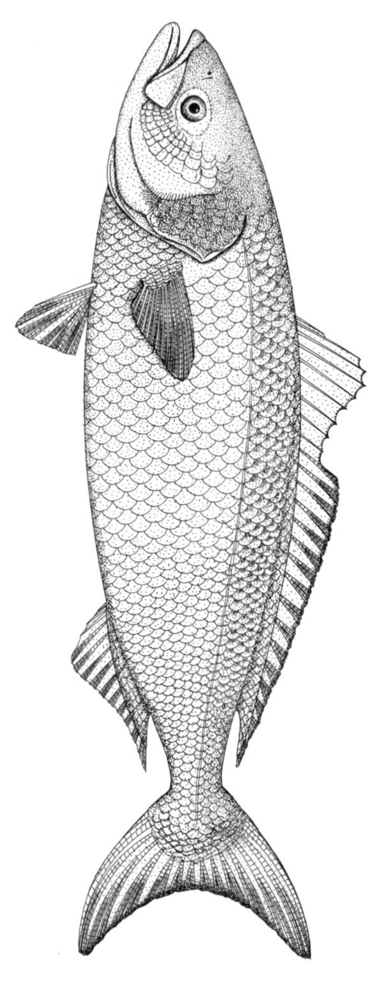

HĀPUKUPUKU, KŌHERE, KŌPŪHURI, KŌUKAUKA, KŌWAITAU, KŌWEREWERE, KOPAPA, KORIA, KŪNGONGINGONGI, PŪAWAI, TĀHURI, TAPURUPURU, TĀROTO

KAHAWAI

Arripis trutta

Description: The kahawai is silvery white on the flanks and blue to green on the upper back with numerous dark spots and speckles. It is white underneath and the pectoral fins are yellowish. Its body is elongate and fusiform. The large mouth is slightly upturned and reaches to below about mid-eye. The dorsal fin is sail-like with nine slender spines followed by a long, low soft-rayed portion. The caudal fin is deeply forked. The pectoral fins are small and pointed, above the pelvic fins which are about the same size. The anal fin is short, below the back of the dorsal fin. Maximum size is 89cm total length.

Distribution in Aotearoa: Widespread from Rangitāhua Kermadec Islands to around Aotearoa and Rēkohu Wharekauri Chatham Islands. It is less common in the far south of Te Waipounamu South Island, where it is more often seen during the summer months. A second, larger species (*Arripis xylabion*) with a bigger tail straggles south from Rangitāhua into northern waters around Te Ika-a-Māui North Island.

Habitat: Pelagic, along the coasts, into estuaries and the lower reaches of rivers, to open ocean in 0 to 233m depth.

Curator's notes: This species is sometimes called 'the people's fish' because of its abundance and ease of capture. They will frequently school with trevally (*Pseudocaranx georgianus*, page 63) of similar size. Fish kept for eating need to be bled, gutted, and chilled quickly on capture, otherwise the quality degrades. Although there are numerous Māori names (sometimes reflecting different stages), kahawai has become the one most used throughout Aotearoa.

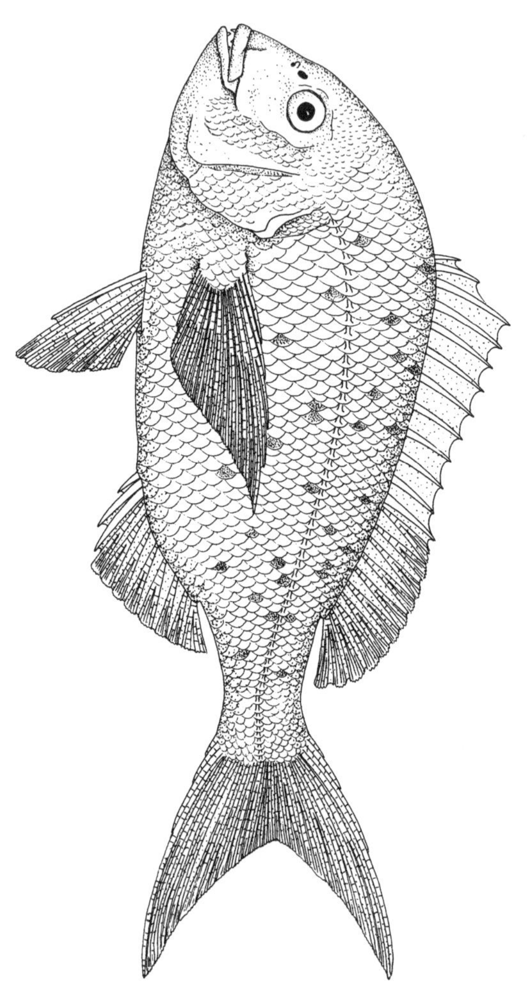

KARATĪ, KOUAREA, KOUREA, PARATETE, PARATOHE, PATATĪ, PEPE TAMURE, TĀMURE

SNAPPER

Chrysophrys auratus

Description: The snapper is an iridescent pink to red with brilliant blue spots, grading to white on the belly. Its body is oval, somewhat compressed. The mouth is short, extending to below the front of the eyes, and has rounded, peg-shaped teeth. The dorsal fin has 12 to 13 strong spines and 9 to 10 soft rays. The caudal fin is wide and forked. The pectoral fins are falcate, over the pelvic fins. The anal fin is of moderate length, under the rear of the dorsal fin. Maximum size is 1.3m standard length.

Distribution in Aotearoa: Found around the coast, more abundant in the north. Two other snapper species have been recorded, but these seem to be stragglers and have not established in our waters. Listed by the IUCN as Least Concern, with stable populations.

Habitat: Found in estuaries, on reefs and off sandy beaches at depths of up to 280m. It follows the saltwater layer of rising tides up the lower reaches of rivers to feed.

Curator's notes: This fish species was of great importance to early Māori, reflected in the numerous different names for different sizes and stages. Like trevally (*Pseudocaranx georgianus*, page 63), large snapper often develop Tilly bones, especially at the crest of the head, which gives very large specimens a hump-headed appearance. This seems to be more commonly seen in Australian populations. Large snapper are important for controlling numbers of kina and paddle crabs. Large individuals are common in the Cape Rodney-Okakari Point Marine Reserve near Leigh, where the urchin barrens (areas bare of kelp owing to grazing pressure) have subsequently disappeared. Stocks in some areas such as Mohua Golden Bay have been enhanced by the release of hatchery spawned and reared juveniles.

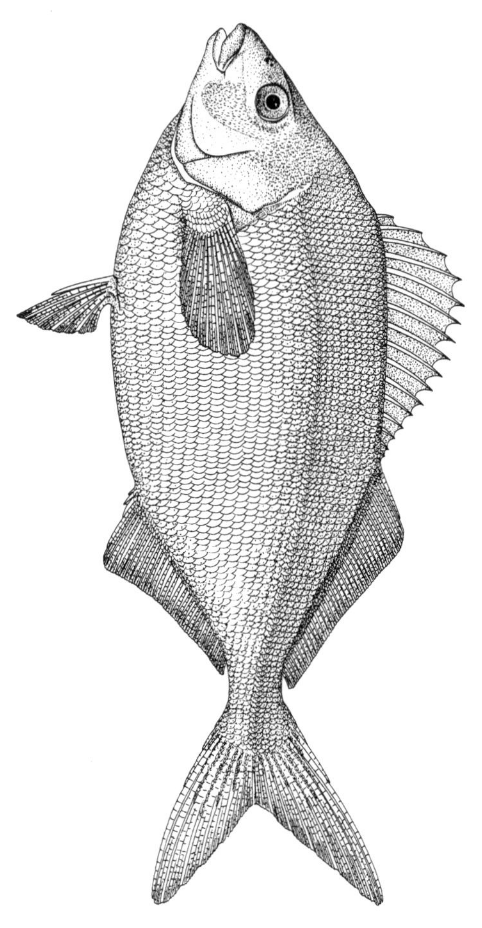

MOKI
BLUE MOKI

Latridopsis cilaris

Description: The blue moki is a silvery blue-grey, fading to a lighter blue on the flanks and off-white on the belly. Its body is ovaloid and compressed. The mouth is small, not extending beyond the eyes, with thick lips. The dorsal fin is long with 16 to 17 strong spines and 37 to 43 soft rays; the caudal fin is forked. The pectoral fins are lobate, and the pelvic fins are positioned under the distal third of the pectoral. The anal fin is about as long as the soft dorsal fin. Maximum size is 80cm total length.

Distribution in Aotearoa: An endemic species, widespread around the coast from off Manawatāwhi Three Kings to Motu Maha Auckland Islands and east to Rēkohu Wharekauri Chatham Islands. Records from Rangitāhua Kermadec Islands need confirmation.

Habitat: Found off the sea bottom around the coast in 0 to 160m depth. They can form large schools, especially during spawning.

Curator's notes: These are curious fish that are attracted to shiny objects, making them easy to spear. Juveniles have a unique paperfish larval stage, with a sharp belly keel (edge), which can last for up to a year. Adults feed on benthic invertebrates; they will suck up sand and retain the prey while spitting out the sediment. It is a commercial and popular recreational species. A small population was seen for a while around Hobart Harbour in Tasmania, which probably came over as juveniles in a ship's sea chest. They eventually died out without forming a viable population. An Australian species, the copper moki (*Latridopsis forsteri*), sometimes straggles to Aotearoa and will school with blue moki.

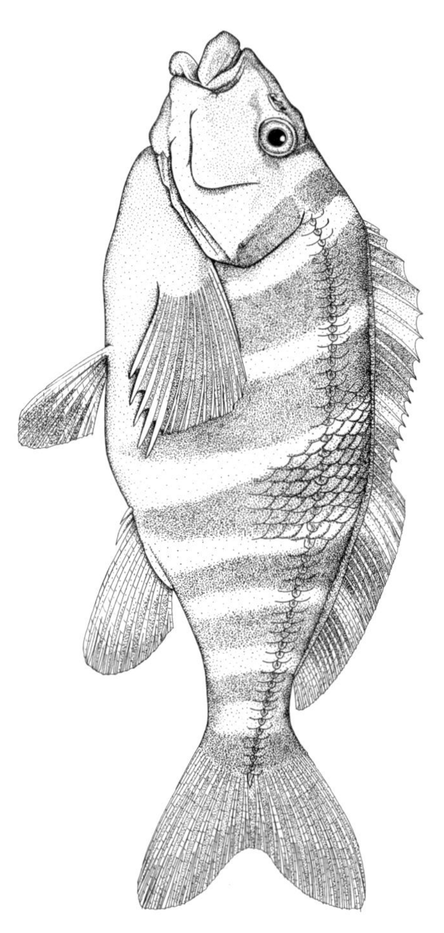

EHOUHOUAMU, MANUA, MARATEA, MARATIA, NANUA, NANUA POUNAMU, NGUTERE

RED MOKI

Chirodactylus spectabilis

Description: This fish has dark reddish-brown mottling on the head, and the body is crossed by six to eight broad dark-red bands and is pale pink to off-white in between, and paler on the belly. Its body is ovaloid and compressed. The mouth is slightly tilted down and small with thick lips, not extending to the eyes. The dorsal fin is long with 17 to 18 strong spines and 25 to 27 soft rays. The caudal fin is forked, with rounded lobes. The pectoral fins are lobate with thickened extended lower rays, and the pelvic fins are positioned under the distal third of the pectoral. The anal fin is short and sail-like, positioned under the forward part of the soft dorsal fin. Maximum size is 70cm total length.

Distribution in Aotearoa: Found around the coast from Te Tai Tokerau Northland to Te Ara a Kiwa Foveaux Strait, and east to Rēkohu Wharekauri Chatham Islands.

Habitat: Usually solitary, found on reefs, especially ones with ledges, gullies and larger caves, in 1 to 54m depth.

Curator's notes: Because of their passive nature and curiosity, red moki have been very heavily depleted in some areas by spearfishing. Fortunately, there is an unofficial moratorium on taking them and numbers have recovered strongly. In some areas they are not allowed to be caught. As red moki are not especially good to eat, they are best watched and left alone. They can be very long-lived, up to 90 years. Their feeding method is similar to that of the blue moki (*Latridopsis cilaris*, page 73).

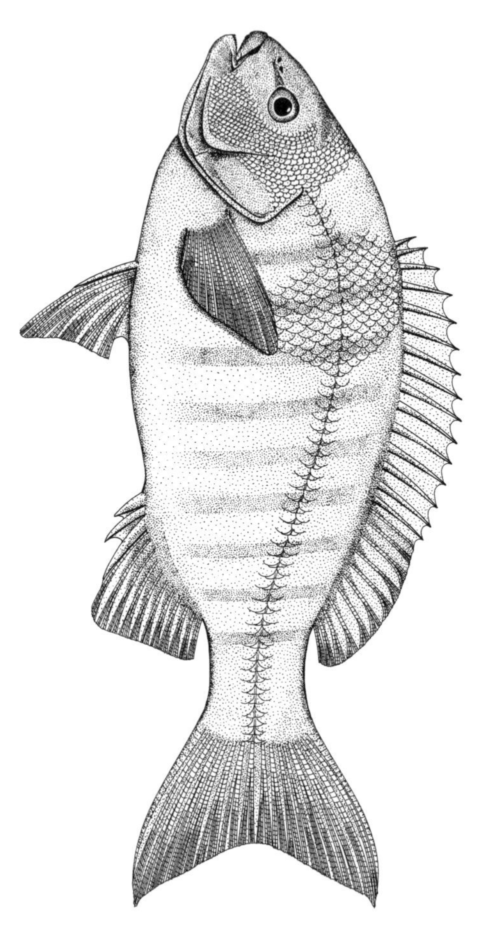

KOPĪPIRO, MURITEA, NGĀOHEOHE, PARAKOKA

PORORE

Girella tricuspidata

Description: This fish is silvery to dark grey with 9 to 12 thin dark-brown lines crossing the body and a paler belly. Its body is oval, with a short, rounded, slightly compressed head with round eyes. The small mouth is slightly tilted down and has small teeth with three points each. It has a single dorsal fin with 13 to 15 spines and 10 to 13 soft rays. The tail is broad and lunate. The pectoral fins are lobate. The anal fin is small and angular, positioned under the soft rear part of the dorsal fin. Maximum size is 39cm standard length, but there are records of porore reaching 60cm.

Distribution in Aotearoa: Around Te Ika-a-Māui North Island, with scattered records from the Whakatū Nelson–Te Tauihu-o-te-waka Marlborough Sounds region.

Habitat: Found in estuaries, mangrove swamps, harbours and coastal reefs, in 1 to 15m depth.

Curator's notes: Porore can occur in huge schools of up to several hundred, but they are shy and difficult to approach. They feed on a wide variety of invertebrates and seaweed. This is another species where a Māori name has been adopted over earlier European ones such as 'blackfish' and 'black bream'. They are reported to be good to eat but need to be quickly gutted and chilled to prevent spoilage. Their conservation status is 'Unknown', but their reliance on estuaries and mangrove swamps (especially the latter) does put them at some risk, as these habitats are themselves diminishing or are being degraded.

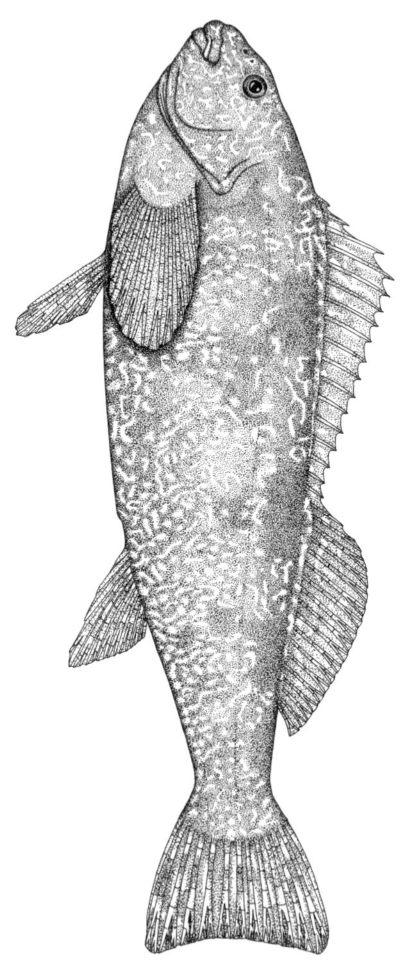

KATIRIMU, KAWIKAWI, KEKE, KEHE, KOEAE, NGEHE

MARBLEFISH

Aplodactylus arctidens

Description: The marblefish is dark olive green with paler spots and reticulations (net-like patterns). Its body is elongate, tapering and becoming more compressed towards the tail; it has a rounded, short head. The mouth is small and oriented downwards, with a fleshy projecting upper lip. The dorsal fin is long, with 15 to 17 strong spines forming a wedge-shaped outline, becoming shorter after the third or fourth, followed by 16 to 18 soft rays. The caudal fin is broad and slightly lunate. The pectoral fins are large and bluntly pointed with the lower rays thickened, positioned over the angular pelvic fins. The anal fin is short and sail-like, positioned under the soft part of the dorsal. Its scales are small, embedded in a leathery skin. Maximum size is 57cm standard length.

Distribution in Aotearoa: Widespread, more common around Te Waipounamu South Island. It occurs east to Rēkohu Wharekauri Chatham Islands and around Tini Heke Snares Islands.

Habitat: Reefs with thick algae cover, especially red algae, in 0 to 20m depth.

Curator's notes: Marblefish are extremely curious and will closely approach a diver before darting away. At rest, they sit facing the surge, splaying their pectoral fins out with the thickened lower rays in contact with the sea floor. Māori prized this fish as good to eat, but only at certain times of the year. Their diet, rich in algae, can taint the flesh with a strong iodine flavour, which has made them unpopular to eat. In the wild, marblefish are almost exclusively herbivores, but they can be encouraged to eat mussels in captivity. They are most active at dusk and dawn.

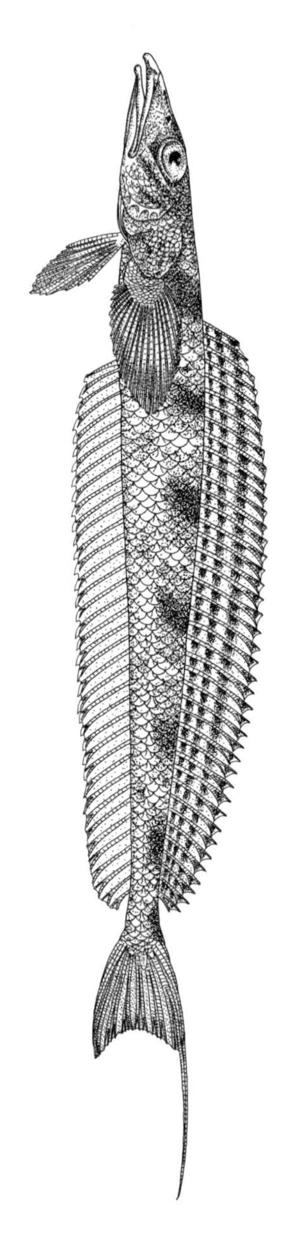

KOHIKOHI
OPALFISH

Hemerocoetes monopterygius

Description: The kohikohi is coloured in mottled browns and creams, with seven dark saddles across the upper body. It has opalescent blue flashes as spots along the body, pelvic fins, tips of the anal fin and on the caudal fin. Its head and body are long, slender and rounded in cross-section, with the head and snout slightly depressed. The snout is long, and the mouth slightly tilted downwards and long, extending past the front of the eyes. It has large eyes on the upper head, with a flap of skin over the upper pupil. The dorsal fin is long and high, comprising 38 to 43 soft rays. The tail is lunate, with the upper fin rays much longer than the lower on mature males. The pelvic fins are long and lobate, positioned ahead of, and the same shape as, the pectoral fins. The anal fin is like the dorsal. Maximum size is 21.8cm standard length.

Distribution in Aotearoa: An endemic species, widespread around the coast from off Otou North Cape to the Snares Shelf, and east to Rēkohu Wharekauri Chatham Islands.

Habitat: Benthic on sandy to shelly-cobble bottoms, usually in 0 to 50m depth.

Curator's notes: There are five species of opalfish around Aotearoa, generally requiring a microscope to identify. Divers on shell hash and cobble bottoms will see this fish darting away, having relied on camouflage to remain unnoticed. They will take a small baited hook, but catching them is purely for novelty value, or for keeping in a marine aquarium. This was one of the fish species caught during Captain James Cook's first voyage, at Astronomer Point in Ata Whenua Fiordland, and is among the earliest to be given a scientific name.

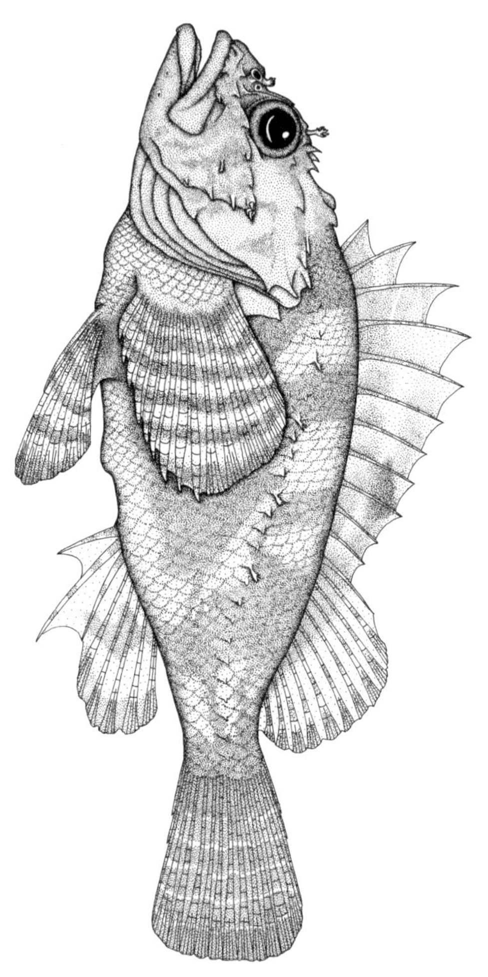

SCORPIONFISH

Scorpaena papillosa

Description: The scorpionfish is vividly mottled red to crimson and brown. It is oval in shape, with a deep body, tapering and becoming compressed towards the tail. The head is cavernous, with a very large mouth, extending beyond the slightly oval eyes, which are high on the head. The head is covered with sharp bony ridges and spines. The dorsal fin is long, with 12 thick, sharp spines and 9 to 10 soft rays. The caudal fin is rounded. The pectoral fins are very large, with most rays thickened, and the pelvic fins are positioned directly beneath. The anal fin is short, positioned under the soft part of the dorsal fin. Maximum size is 22cm standard length.

Distribution: An endemic species, very widespread around the coast from Manawatāwhi Three Kings Islands to the southern Snares Shelf, and east to Rēkohu Wharekauri Chatham Islands.

Habitat: On reefs in 0 to 188m depth, usually less than 50m.

Curator's notes: The spines of this fish, especially the dorsal spines, are T-shaped with venomous tissue in the groove. Someone experiencing a puncture wound from a scorpionfish will feel excruciating pain, localised swelling and nausea. In severe cases, from a large specimen, it can also affect vision. Treatment is to immerse the puncture site in water as hot as can be tolerated. The puncture site will remain tender and itchy for several days. To remove one from a hook, place a thumb in its mouth and hold it by the lower jaw. One of three scorpionfish known from Aotearoa, this species is the most widespread, common, and the smallest. Usually hunting at night, they employ a 'hop and wait' strategy, sensing any currents produced by crabs and small fishes.

MATUAWHAPUKU, POHUIAKAROA, POHUIKAROA, PUAIHAKARUA

JOCK STEWART

Helicolenus percoides

Description: This fish is coloured in highly variable reds, pinks, oranges and browns. Five bands cross the body, the one under the soft dorsal fin being Y-shaped. It is oval in shape with a moderately deep body. The mouth is large, extending to below the back of the large, round eyes on the upper head. The head has spines that are small and/or flattened. The long dorsal fin has 12 spines and 12 soft rays. The caudal fin is truncate to slightly lunate. The pectoral fins are large and fan-shaped, the lower half comprising thickened separate rays with the pelvic fins directly underneath. The anal fin is short under the soft part of the dorsal. Maximum size is 43cm standard length.

Distribution in Aotearoa: Found all around the coast and offshore, including offshore ridges and islands.

Habitat: On reefs to shell and cobble bottoms, in 0 to 350m depth.

Curator's notes: One of two species in Aotearoa. They can only be distinguished genetically as identifying them otherwise is very difficult. This is a popular recreational species that has accumulated a plethora of local common names in Aotearoa and Australia. Their cavernous mouths can not only accommodate large hooks, but also act as a drag chute, giving the angler the impression that they have caught a much larger fish. Large specimens are very good to eat, although the fillet can be small. Unlike the scorpionfish (*Scorpaena papillosa*, page 83), the spines do not appear to be venomous. Jock Stewart also don't appear to have a prolonged pelagic larval stage, so local colour patterns can develop. They can live for over 40 years.

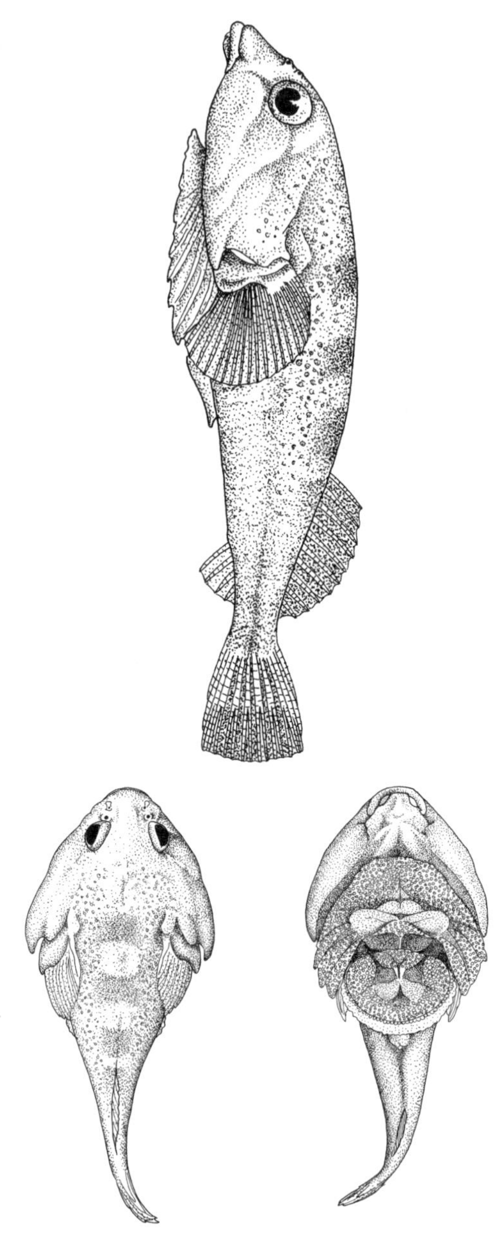

ORANGE CLINGFISH

Diplocrepus punaceus

Description: Despite the common name, the orange clingfish is a translucent greenish brown with darker bands and black speckling; the common name is derived from the colour they appear in preservative. Its eyes have a bright orange rim to the pupil. It is teardrop-shaped, the profile being humped along the back and flat underneath. The mouth is oriented downward, does not extend back below the eyes, and has small, flattened incisor-like teeth in a line. The eyes are high on the head, point forward and slightly up. The dorsal fin is short and towards the tail, comprising soft rays. The caudal fin has a straight edge (truncate) when spread out. The pectoral fins are fan-shaped. The pelvic fins have a complex broad-disc structure. The anal fin is short, positioned under the back of the dorsal fin. This fish has no scales, rather skin with a thick mucus coat. Maximum size is 12cm standard length.

Distribution in Aotearoa: An endemic genus, occuring from Manawatāwhi Three Kings Islands to Rakiura Stewart Island and east to Rēkohu Wharekauri Chatham Islands.

Habitat: Coastal on reefs and on the underside of boulders, from rockpools to a subtidal depth of 15m.

Curator's notes: There is only a single species in the genus. The specialised pelvic fins are used to suck onto rocks, hence the common name for the family – clingfish. The colour mimics the crustose coraline algae in which the fish live. When disturbed, it moves back under the home rock in a series of swift jumps. The body shape and absence of scales is an adaptation to living in areas where surge is common, as the water moves over the fish and does not knock it off the rock. Similar-shaped teeth on a South American species were described as being used to prise small snails off rocks before eating them. Males guard eggs laid under home rocks.

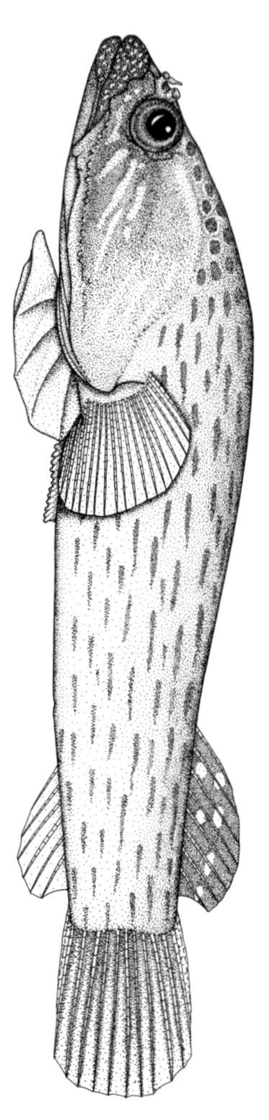

MŌHAKIHAKI, MOHIARU, MŌWHAKIWHAKI

LUMPFISH

Trachelochismus pinnulatus

Description: The lumpfish is coloured greenish brown with fine, darker horizontal speckling; some specimens have vertical pale bars. The eyes have a bright yellow to orange rim to the pupil. This fish is teardrop-shaped, the profile being slightly humped over the back and flat underneath, and the upper head flattened across the snout. The mouth has thick lips, extends to below the eyes, and has small, curved conical teeth. The eyes are high on the head, pointing forward and slightly up. The dorsal fin is short, positioned towards the rear of the body and comprises soft rays. The caudal fin is truncate when spread out. The pectoral fins are fan-shaped. The pelvic fins form a complex broad-disc structure on the belly, acting as a sucking disc to help anchor the fish to surfaces. The anal fin is short, positioned under the dorsal fin. This fish has no scales, rather skin with a thick mucus coat. Maximum size is 9cm standard length.

Distribution in Aotearoa: An endemic genus. Lumpfish are widespread around the coast from Manawatāwhi Three Kings Islands to Tini Heke Snares Islands, and east to Rēkohu Wharekauri Chatham Islands.

Habitat: Undersides of rocks and boulders in rockpools to 60m depth.

Curator's notes: The three species in the genus are primarily distinguished by the pattern of dimples across the sucking disc. Males guard a nest site under rocks, with several females laying the eggs. Their behaviour is similar to the orange clingfish (*Diplocrepus punaceus*, page 87). A larger mouth armed with small, fang-like teeth allows the lumpfish to prey on bigger animals than the orange clingfish, such as porcelain crabs. The colour pattern is closer to green algae than the crustose coraline reds seen on the orange clingfish.

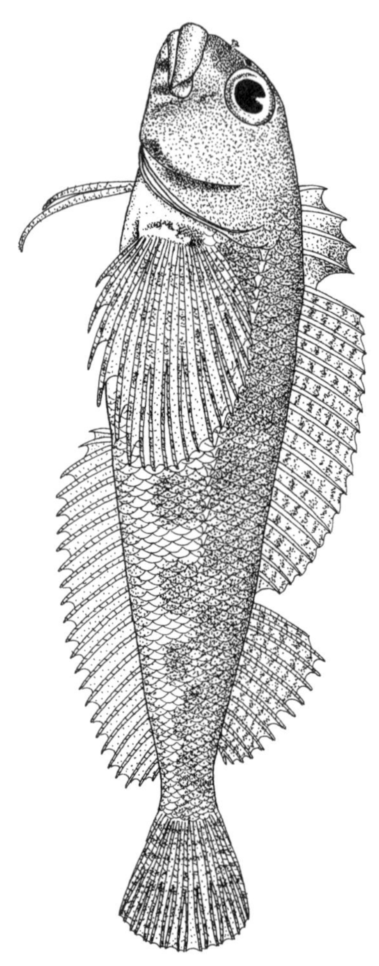

TWISTER

Bellapiscis medius

Description: A mottled brown to greenish colour, matching stones and algae in the background, the twister has a series of light and dark checkerboard patterns along its lower flanks. Males become darker in the breeding season. It has a slender, tapering body and a wedge-shaped head. The large mouth, with thick lips, extends to midway under the large eyes on the upper head. The first dorsal fin is short and low with four slender spines, the second long with 14 to 17 spines, the third sail-like with 10 to 14 soft rays. The tail is rounded. The pectoral fins are large and fan-like, with its lower rays thickened and partially separated. The pelvic fins are narrow and long, positioned under the base of the pectoral fins. Maximum size is 8.5cm standard length.

Distribution in Aotearoa: An endemic species, the twister is found around coastal Aotearoa, east to Rēkohu Wharekauri Chatham Islands. It is absent from offshore rock stacks and smaller islands.

Habitat: Found in the highest pools on the shoreline that are regularly flushed by waves at high tide, or to a maximum subtidal depth of 5m.

Curator's notes: One of two species in the genus, this triplefin is a high-tide-pool specialist. They can tolerate greater extremes of temperature and dissolved oxygen. Their colours and patterning are excellent camouflage against the turfing algae found in high-tide pools. This is one of 27 species of triplefin found in our region, all endemic, making them a 'species flock'. This is very uncommon in the marine environment and reflects New Zealand's long isolation from other land masses.

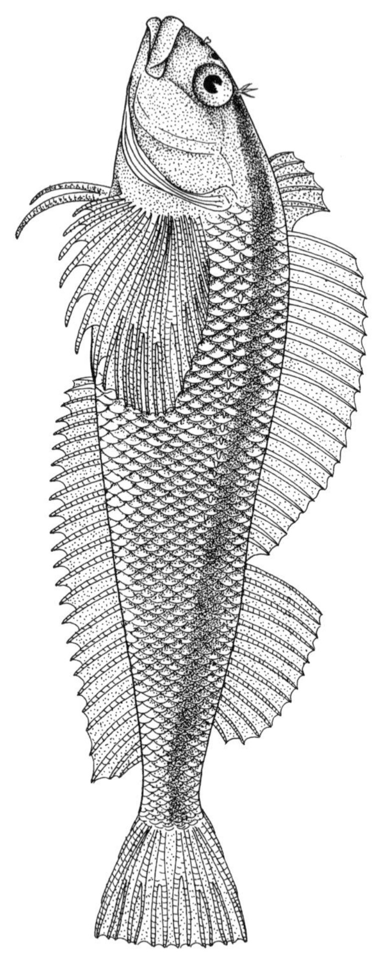

COMMON TRIPLEFIN

Forsterygion lapillum

Description: This fish has three different colour morphs, all sharing a black streak along the flank from behind the eye to the base of the tail (still discernible on the dark morph), and scale pockets with black edges creating a lattice-work pattern. Males become darker in the breeding season. It has a slender, tapering body and a wedge-shaped head. The large mouth has thick lips and extends to midway under the large eyes on the upper head. The first dorsal fin is short and low with 5 to 7 slender spines, the second is long with 19 to 22 spines and the third sail-like with 11 to 13 soft rays. The tail is rounded. The pectoral fins are large and fan-like, the lower rays thickened and partially separated. The pelvic fins are narrow and long; the anal fin is also long. Maximum size is 8.4cm standard length.

Distribution in Aotearoa: An endemic species, found around Aotearoa from Otou North Cape to Rakiura Stewart Island, but absent from Rēkohu Wharekauri Chatham Islands and smaller offshore rock stacks and islands.

Habitat: Extremely widespread in estuaries, coastal reefs, rockpools and rocky beaches, in 0 to 10m depth.

Curator's notes: In spite of its common name, this fish wasn't recognised as a distinct species until 1989; before then, the scientific name *Tripterygion capito* was incorrectly applied. Having three distinct colour forms (often in the same area) added to historical confusion. Juveniles are common in rockpools in late spring, where they can be prey for seabirds. Specimens were translocated, probably in ship sea chests, to Port Philip Bay, Victoria, sometime in the 1990s. The current status of the Australian population is unknown. After the 2016 Kaikōura earthquake they were the first triplefins to re-establish along the coast.

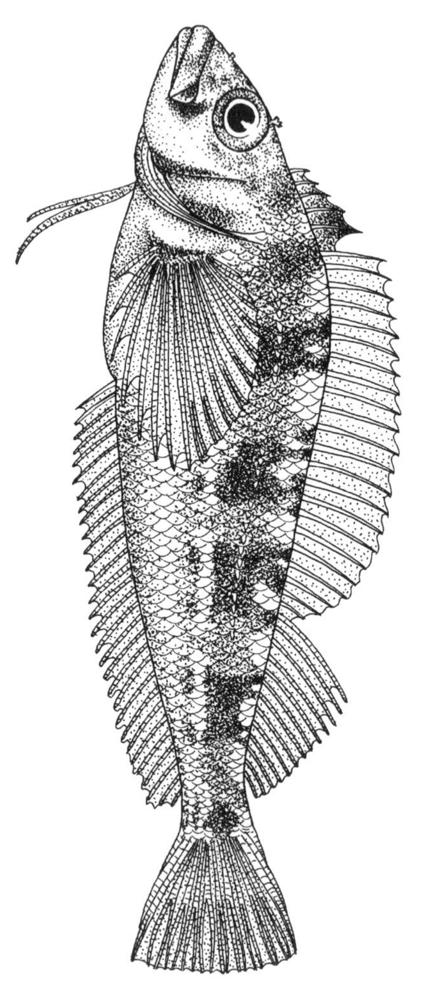

VARIABLE TRIPLEFIN

Forsterygion varium

Description: The variable triplefin is a creamy brown fish with a series of dusky bars and saddles crossing the upper body to mid-flank. The tips of the first and second dorsal fins are iridescent blue. Males become darker in the breeding season. It has a slender, tapering body and a wedge-shaped head. The large mouth, with thick lips, extends to midway under the large eyes on the upper head. The first dorsal fin is short and low with five to seven slender spines, the second long with 22 to 25 spines, and the third sail-like with 13 to 17 soft rays. The tail is rounded. The pectoral fins are large and fan-like, the lower rays thickened and partially separated. The pelvic fins are narrow and long. Maximum size is 13.3cm standard length.

Distribution in Aotearoa: An endemic genus. Variable triplefins are widespread around the coast from Te Tai Tokerau Northland to Rakiura Stewart Island and Tini Heke Snares, Motu Maha Auckland and Rēkohu Wharekauri Chatham Islands.

Habitat: Mid-tide pools to subtidal on reefs and rocky beaches to 33m depth. Extremely common among larger algae species.

Curator's notes: Collected at Ships Cove in Te Tauihu-o-te-waka Marlborough Sounds during Captain James Cook's second expedition, this triplefin was scientifically described in 1801. The scientific and common names probably arose because early scientists didn't appreciate the large number of species they were collecting and believed them to all be one 'variable' species. A number of specimens were accidentally translocated to Kangaroo Bay, Tasmania, probably in a shipment of oysters, where they appear to have established locally. Initially described as a distinct species, they were recognised as the same as the variable triplefin in 1989. The Tasmanian population have protected species status.

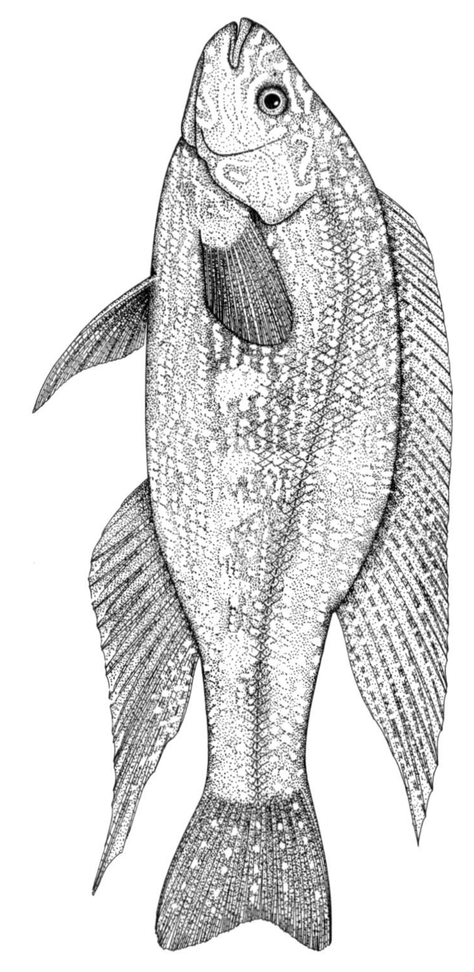

KŌEAEA, MARARE, MARARI, MARARĪ, MATOHE, RARĪ, TARAO

BUTTERFISH

Odax pullus

Description: The colour of this fish is highly variable. Juveniles are either butter yellow or brilliant green with a broken line of silvery white from the mouth along the mid-flank. Females become more mottled green, while males have iridescent blue and purple fins and blue lines over the head. Its body is fusiform, with head bluntly pointed. The mouth is small, with fused cutting plates of teeth in both jaws. The eyes are round and high on the head. The dorsal fin is long and sail-like with 19 to 21 fine spines and 12 to 14 soft rays. The caudal fin is emarginate to lunate. The pectoral fins are bluntly pointed. The anal fin is short, positioned under the rear of the dorsal fin. Scales are small and embedded. Maximum size is 70cm standard length.

Distribution in Aotearoa: An endemic genus. Widespread around the coast from Otou North Cape to Tini Heke Snares Islands, and east to Rēkohu Wharekauri Chatham Islands. Some have been seen from Moutere Hauriri Bounty and Motu Mahue Antipodes Islands.

Habitat: On reefs where their favoured brown algae occur, in 0 to 30m depth.

Curator's notes: A popular recreational fish, caught mainly by spear or set net. They quickly become wary of divers. In the Te Whanganui a-Tara Wellington area numbers have recovered strongly in the Taputeranga Marine Reserve, where they show no fear of divers or swimmers. Although considered vegetarian, they also consume large numbers of algal-dwelling molluscs. The juveniles are so different in shape and colour to adults that they were originally considered to be a separate genus. This species changes sex from female to male with age. An older common name, 'greenbone', refers to the bright blue-green colour of the skeleton.

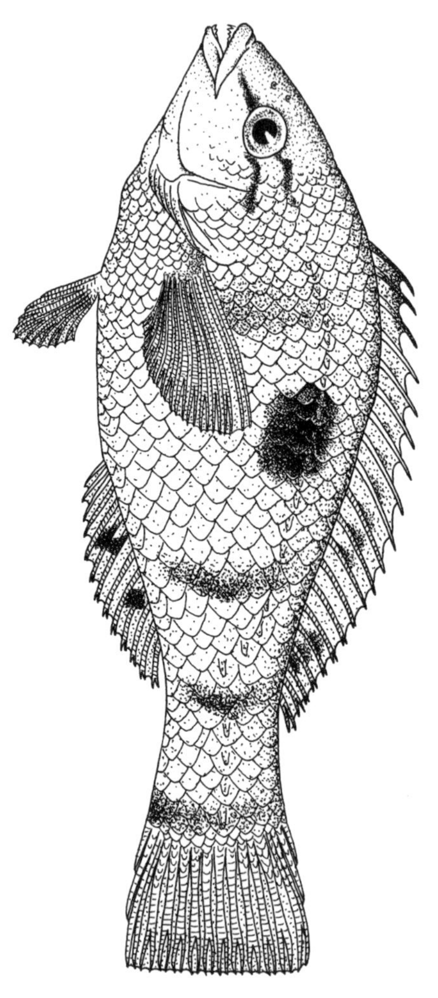

PAEKIRIKIRI, PAKETI, PAKIRIKIRI, TĀNGĀNGĀ, TĀNGAHANGAHA
SPOTTY

Notolabrus celidotus

Description: The spotty varies in colour depending on age and sex. They are commonly seen with brown and yellow on the fins and a large dark brown spot on the flank, with short bars crossing the body after the spot. Juveniles on seagrass are a brilliant green, but a metallic bronze in brown algae. Mature males become bluish green, the spot breaking up to a more horizontal mark; they have iridescent blue lines on the head. Its body is oval, slightly compressed. The short mouth has large conical teeth and a large upper lip. The eyes are round and high on the head. The dorsal fin is long with 9 spines and 11 soft rays. The caudal fin is emarginate to truncate. The pectoral fins are large and wedge-shaped. The anal fin is moderately long. Scales are large. Maximum size is 24cm standard length.

Distribution in Aotearoa: An endemic species, widespread around the coast from Otou North Cape to Rakiura Stewart Island, and east to Rēkohu Wharekauri Chatham Islands.

Habitat: Estuaries, harbours and coastal reefs, from 0 to 145m depth, most commonly seen above 20m. They prefer more sheltered waters so are absent from Manawatāwhi Three Kings and Tini Heke Snares Islands.

Curator's notes: Spotties are extremely abundant, especially in sheltered harbours. Like all wrasses they have a complex sex life, with some specimens changing from female to male at about 20cm standard length. The male will hold an area and a harem of females and become very aggressive towards other fishes. If he is removed, the largest resident female will often transition to male. Some people consider larger fishes to be excellent eating.

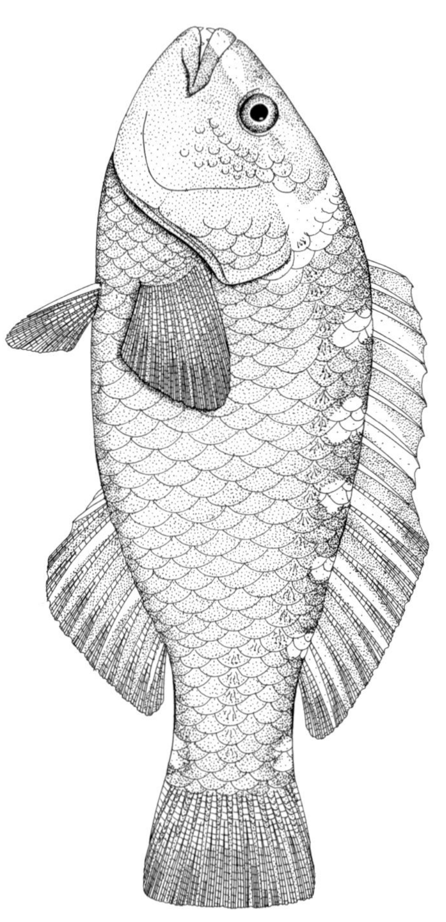

TĀNGAHANGAHA
BANDED WRASSE

Notolabrus fucicola

Description: The tāngahangaha varies in colour depending on age and sex. Small specimens are mottled green to red. Mature males are blue to blue green with five or six dark purplish bars crossing the flanks onto the dorsal and anal fins, which have a dark and off-white to yellowish pattern. Its body is oval and slightly compressed. The short mouth has large conical teeth and a large upper lip. The eyes are round and high on the head. The dorsal fin is long with 9 spines and 11 soft rays. The caudal fin is emarginate to truncate. The pectoral fins are large and wedge-shaped. The anal fin is moderately long. Scales are large. Maximum size is 50cm standard length.

Distribution on Aotearoa: Widespread around the coast from Manawatāwhi Three Kings Islands to Tini Heke Snares Islands, and east to Rēkohu Wharekauri Chatham Islands.

Habitat: Found on rocky reefs and regions with abundant algae, usually in 0 to 15m depth.

Curator's notes: Unlike spotties (*Notolabrus celidotus*, page 99), tāngahangaha are found around offshore reefs. They are capable of breaking bits off pāua and large mussels for food. Banded wrasses will readily take a baited hook and are strong fighters, but are best released alive as they are not very good to eat, being soft with a somewhat insipid flavour. Male banded wrasse are very intolerant of other males and will engage in violent fighting to maintain their territory and harem.

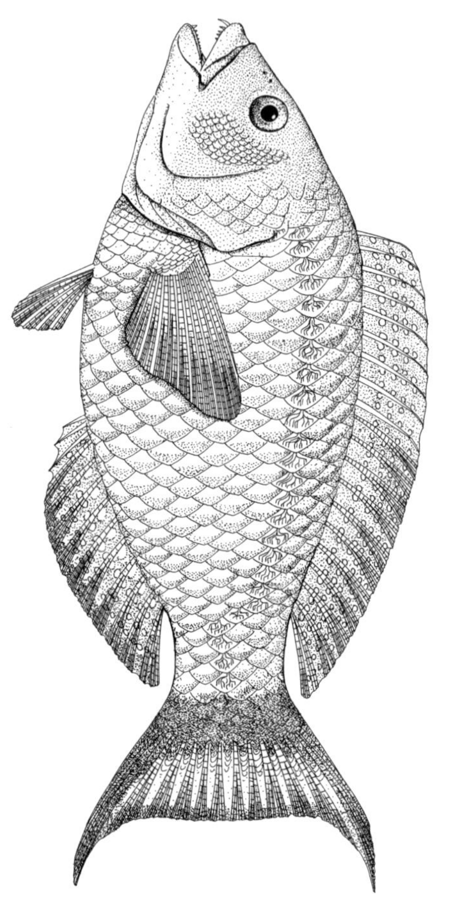

PAU, PAWAIWHAKARUA, PŪWAIWHAKARUA
SCARLET WRASSE

Pseudolabrus miles

Description: The scarlet wrasse varies in colour with age and sex. Small specimens are red on the upper head and flank, with horizontal red lines on the mid to lower flank. They are greenish yellow in between, and white on the lower head and body around the pectoral fins. There is a dark blotch before the tail. The head of mature males is almost entirely red; the red on the body breaks up to scale pockets, and the black before the tail becomes a solid bar. Dorsal and anal fins of both sexes are lavender with yellow-green spots, the tips iridescent blue. The red colour becomes a greenish grey at depth as a camouflage. Its body is oval and slightly compressed. The mouth has large conical teeth and a large upper lip. The eyes are round and high on the head. The dorsal fin is long with 9 spines and 11 soft rays. The caudal fin is emarginate, becoming lunate on mature males (upper filament slightly longer). The pectoral fins are large and wedge-shaped. The anal fin is moderately long. Scales are large. Maximum size is 35cm standard length.

Distribution in Aotearoa: Endemic, widespread around the coast from Manawatāwhi Three Kings Islands to Tini Heke Snares Islands and the southern Snares Shelf, and east to Rēkohu Wharekauri Chatham Islands.

Habitat: Bottom-dwellers, on reefs with broken rocks and crevices and encrusting invertebrates (preferring areas without seaweed). They are found at 4 to 40m depth, more commonly below 10m.

Curator's notes: This is our most attractive wrasse. Mature males are brighter in colour than females. Juveniles have been observed acting as cleaner fish. When alarmed, these fish will sometimes bury themselves in sand or under rocks. The author once observed a large male repeatedly striking at a small octopus that had ventured into its territory.

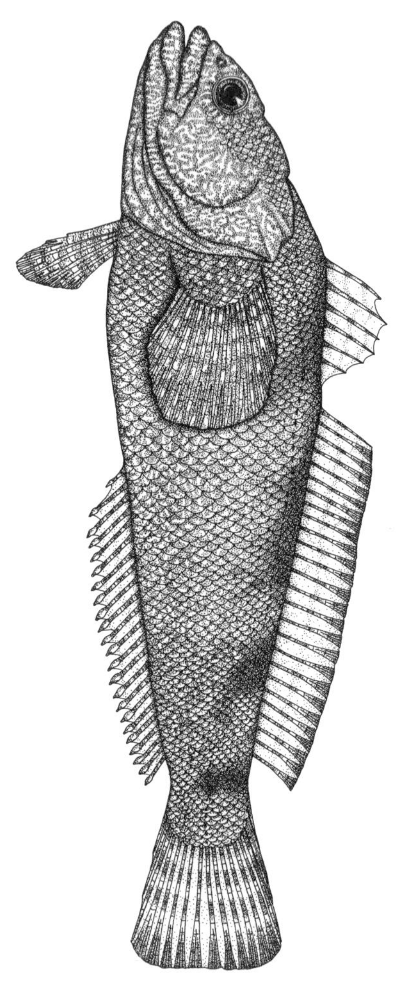

MĀORI CHIEF

Notothenia angustata

Description: This fish, when mature, is olive green to blue green, with yellow spots over the head, body and fins, and a complex pattern of darker spots and lines over the head. Juveniles are a metallic bronze. It is elongate with a large cavernous head. The mouth is large, extending to the front of the eyes, with thick lips. The eyes are small, round, high on the head and facing slightly forward, with a strong bony ridge above. The first dorsal fin is small and sail-like, with four to seven flexible spines, the second higher than the first with 27 to 30 soft rays. The caudal fin is rounded. The pectoral fins are very large and fan-like. The anal fin is similar in length and height as the second dorsal fin. Large embedded scales cover the body, while the head is naked. Maximum size is 47cm standard length.

Distribution in Aotearoa: Found from the Wairarapa coast, south to Motu Ihupuku Campbell Islands and east to Rēkohu Wharekauri Chatham Islands. More common around Te Waipounamu South Island south of Kaikōura.

Habitat: Benthic, found in large rockpools and on rocky reefs in 0 to 100m depth. Juveniles up to 10cm long are found in surface waters.

Curator's notes: The Māori chief has become much less common in its northern limit, probably due to rising sea temperatures. They are in the same family as the Patagonian toothfish. Being very sluggish, they can be caught by hand when in rockpools. Eclectic in their choice of prey, they will feed on whatever will fit in their mouth. The common name is derived from the tattoo-like markings over the head. Slow-growing, this species is probably easily overfished.

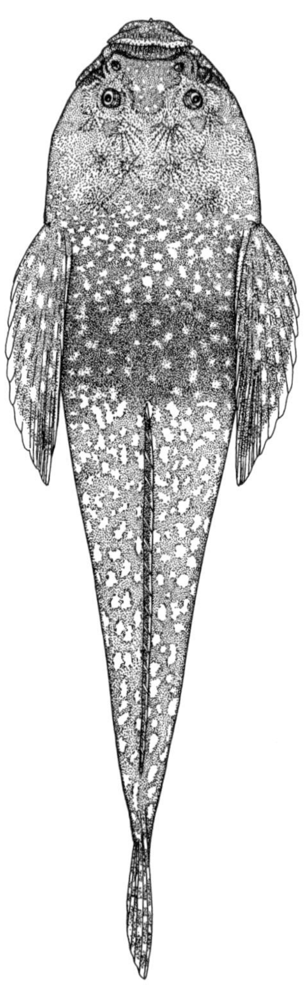

KOUREPOUA, MOAMOA, NGU
SPOTTED STARGAZER

Genyagnus monopterygius

Description: The spotted stargazer is green with brown spots covering the head, upper body and upper pectoral fins. The underside of the head, belly and lower flanks is white. Its body tapers from a broad, flattened head. The large mouth is vertically directed and armed with sharp teeth. The eyes are small and on the top of the head. The single long dorsal fin has no spines and 16 to 20 soft rays. The caudal fin is rounded to truncate. The pectoral fins are very large and fan-like, and lower rays are thickened and separate. The pelvic fins are positioned on the throat. The anal fin is opposite, and about the same size, as the dorsal fin. Maximum size is 45cm standard length.

Distribution in Aotearoa: An endemic species, widespread around the coast from Te Tai Tokerau Northland to Ata Whenua Fiordland.

Habitat: Benthic in estuaries, harbours and bays where there is an abundance of sand, in 0 to 200m depth.

Curator's notes: The very large sharp spine on the upper gill cover can cause a painful wound to the unwary. These fish bury themselves in sand with just their eyes and the upper edge of the mouth showing above a faint coffin-shaped outline in the sand. The frilled mouth lets water in but keeps sand out. They are an ambush predator, with a small fleshy lure off the tongue that draws in unwitting fishes. Prey are inhaled with a rapid expansion of the mouth that can be as quick as 30 milliseconds. This is enabled by a gap in the backbone behind the head that allows the head and mouth to be bent up nearly 90 degrees. The spotted stargazer's highly elastic stomach means it can consume items larger than itself. If disturbed by divers, they can aggressively charge at them, snapping, as the author once discovered.

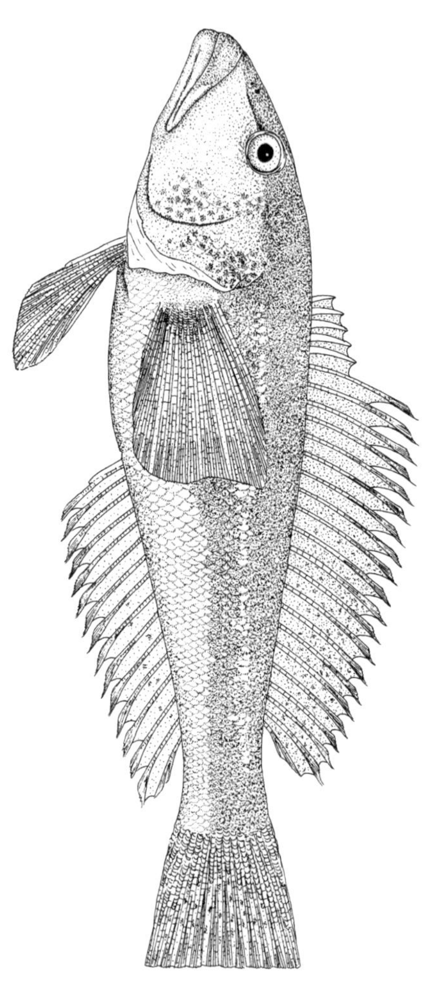

KOPUKOPU, PĀKIRIKIRI, PĀTUTUKI, RĀWARU

BLUE COD

Parapercis colias

Description: Blue cod are born female and can change sex as they mature. They vary in colour depending on age and sex. Smaller specimens (females) are brown over the head and have two broad, broken stripes along their body to the base of the tail. The flanks are pale tan, with indistinct bars extending to the base of the anal fin. Males have the same pattern but are deep blue to blue green. The body is elongate and slightly tapering from a large wedge-shaped head. The large mouth has sharp conical teeth and thick lips, reaching to under the front of the eyes, which are high on the head. The dorsal fin is long with five short spines followed by 20 to 21 longer soft rays. The tail is broad and truncate. The pectoral fins are large and fan-like; the pelvic fins are short, and covered by thickened skin under the gill margin. Maximum size is 60cm standard length.

Distribution in Aotearoa: An endemic species, widespread around the coast from Manawatāwhi Three Kings Islands to Tini Heke Snares Islands, and east to Rēkohu Chatham Islands. It is more abundant in cooler waters.

Habitat: Benthic over a wide range of habitats from reef to sand, in 0 to 200m depth, most commonly in 15 to 150m.

Curator's notes: Blue cod are protogynous hermaphrodites, meaning that they start life as females and change to male with age and increasing size. Sexual maturity occurs at different sizes and ages depending on location. Very curious fish, they will follow divers around to pick up any prey disturbed. Numbers and sizes have increased in the Taputeranga Marine Reserve on Te Whanganui-a-Tara Wellington's south coast. Blue cod can live for over 30 years and is the largest species in the Pinguipedidae family.

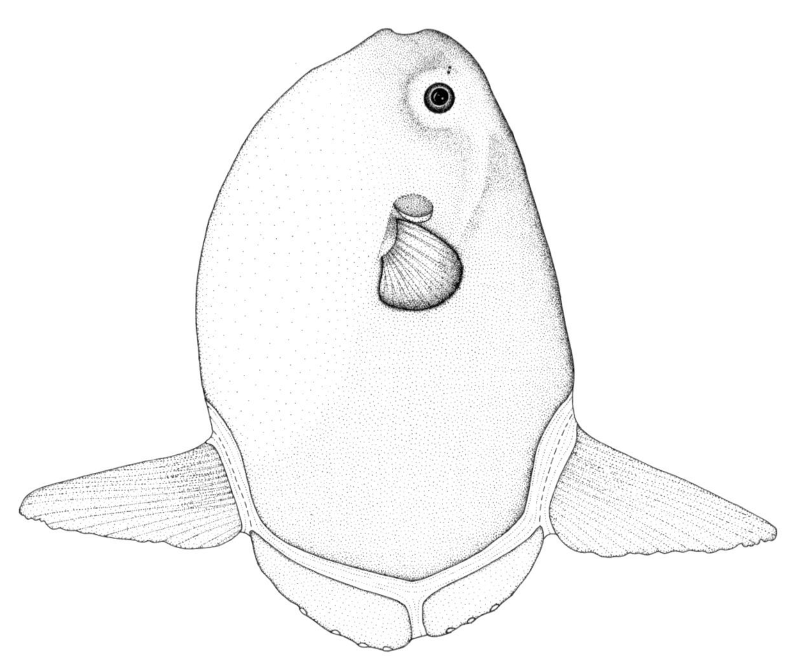

RĀTĀHUIHUI
HOODWINKER SUNFISH

Mola tecta

Description: This fish is brownish grey with irregular off-white spotting and marbling, and is off-white on the belly. Its head and body are oval and compressed. The small mouth has teeth that are fused to form a beak-like structure. The eyes are small and high on the head. The narrow dorsal fin is positioned high on the rear of the body. The tail in this species is replaced by a fleshy rudder-like structure (clavis). The pectoral fins are small and lobe-like; there are no pelvic fins. The anal fin is opposite the dorsal fin and mirrors it in shape and size. Maximum size is at least 2.45m total length.

Distribution in Aotearoa: Although widespread, exact distribution is not fully known.

Habitat: Epipelagic. Maximum depth is unknown.

Curator's notes: The Māori name recorded here is probably just as valid for this species as the other two species in the genus. It is frequently encountered as a beach-cast specimen. The hoodwinker and bump-headed sunfish (*Mola alexandrini*) are the two most common species in waters around Aotearoa. The true sunfish (*Mola mola*) is known only from one record, previously making it the only species known in the genus. Scientists can now distinguish three species. The hoodwinker sunfish was described in 2017.

KŌPŪTŌTARA, KŌPŪWAITŌTARA, NOHU
SOUTHERN BURRFISH

Allomycterus pilatus

Description: The southern burrfish is grey green across the top of the head and body, and bright white elsewhere. Irregular oval yellow blotches with blackish halos appear over the top of the body and extend onto the flanks, being dense around the pectoral fins. Its body is globose. The small mouth has teeth fused into a beak-like structure. The round eyes are very large and on top of the head. The dorsal fin is positioned to the rear of the fish and is sail-like, comprising 15 to 17 soft rays. The caudal fin is rounded. The pectoral fins are wedge-shaped, with the anal fin opposite and the same shape and size as the dorsal; there are no pelvic fins. Both head and body carry large, fixed, erect blade-like spines. Maximum size is 50cm standard length.

Distribution in Aotearoa: Widespread around the coast, more common around Te Ika-a-Māui North Island.

Habitat: Bottom-dwelling, occurring on rocky reefs in 0 to 363m depth.

Curator's notes: Previously, this species was called the porcupinefish, but that common name is more suited to a different genus with longer spines, more commonly found in the tropics. Southern burrfish are often encountered on sandy beaches as trawler discards that have washed ashore. They quickly rot away, leaving behind the leathery swim bladder, which looks like a giant tooth, and the enlarged flattened skin spines, which look like a medieval anti-cavalry weapon called the caltrop. This species may be toxic, like many of its close relatives, and so should never be eaten or fed to pets.

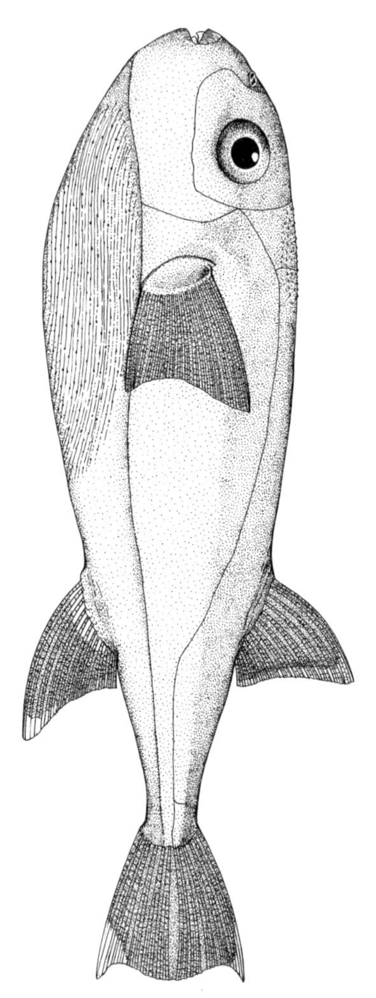

CHEESEMAN'S PUFFER

Lagocephalus cheesemanii

Description: This fish is dark metallic olive green over its dorsal surface and fins, becoming slightly paler on the upper flanks and then silvery, with a bright white belly. The tips of the caudal fin are also white. Its body is elongate and globose, with a bluntly rounded head. The small mouth contains teeth fused into a beak-like structure. The eyes are large and positioned on the sides of the head. The dorsal fin is positioned at the rear and is sail-like, comprising 10 to 15 soft rays. The caudal fin is double emarginate. The pectoral fins are wedge-shaped with a concave margin; there are no pelvic fins. The anal fin is opposite and the same shape and size as the dorsal fin. A diamond-shaped patch of small prickles sits on the top of the head over the eyes, and the belly has pleats and larger prickles. Maximum size is 28.5cm standard length.

Distribution in Aotearoa: Mainly around Te Ika-a-Māui North Island.

Habitat: Bottom-dwelling in coastal regions and estuaries, it is also known to be pelagic, occurring in 0 to 200m depth.

Curator's notes: Amateur ichthyologist Frank Clarke described this puffer from Motouroa, Taranaki, as a new species in 1897. Although his description and drawing were meticulous, the species was not known outside of Aotearoa. This changed in 2016 when a paper was published showing that *Lagocephalus cheesemanii* was widespread throughout the western Pacific Ocean and had other scientific names. As Clarke had published the first name, however, his had priority. The name is dedicated to William Cheeseman who found and sent him the first specimen.

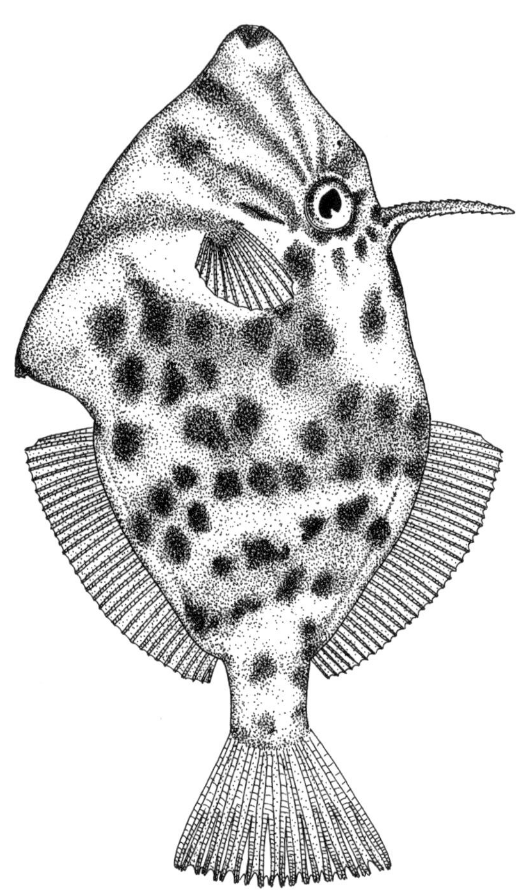

HIRIHIRI, KIRIRĪ, KOKIRIKIRI, KŌKIRI LEATHERJACKET

Meuschenia scaber

Description: This fish varies in colour depending on sex. Females are creamy tan with yellow to near-transparent fins, darker lines radiating from the eye and irregular darker spots over the flank. Males are darker, with a narrow dark bar across the tail. The body and head are diamond-shaped and compressed. The small mouth has teeth that are separate and blade-like. The round eyes are set on the upper head. The first dorsal fin is a strong, sharp serrated spine, the second lies much further to the rear with 32 to 38 soft rays. The caudal fin is rounded to truncate. The pectoral fins are small and angular and there are no pelvic fins. The anal fin is positioned opposite the second dorsal fin. Scales are embedded with an upright point, giving them a sandpaper texture. Maximum size is 33.6cm standard length.

Distribution in Aotearoa: Widespread around the coast including Rangitāhua Kermadec Islands, and east to Rēkohu Wharekauri Chatham Islands. More common around Te Ika-a-Māui North Island.

Habitat: Found on rocky reefs with kelp and abundant encrusting invertebrates, in 1 to 300m depth.

Curator's notes: Leatherjackets feed by scraping invertebrates off rocks using their teeth. If an item is too large, they will utilise 'bite and spit' and repeat this until the prey is small enough to swallow. The main dorsal spine can be fixed in the upright position in a defensive gesture or by males posturing against each other. This is achieved by a smaller spine in front of it locking into a groove of the larger spine. Males will establish a territory and defend it from other males. There is a small recreational and commercial catch.

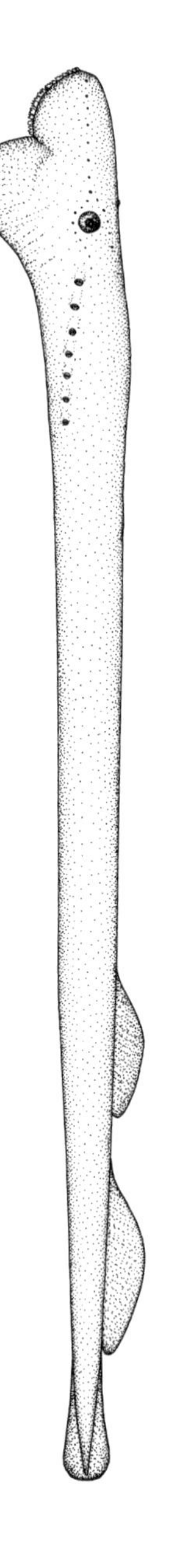

KANAKANA, KANAKANA-WAIRAKI, KOROKORO, NGANANGANA, PIA, PIHAPIHARAU, PIHARU, PIPIHARAU, PUHIKOROKORO, TUNA KOROKORO, UTE, WAIRAKI, WAITUERE

LAMPREY

Geotria australis

Description: Both juveniles and maturing lamprey are silvery with an iridescent blue to blue-green stripe along the upper body. Mature adults are greenish grey. Its body is eel-shaped, rounded at the head end and compressed at the rear. The mouth is a circular hole not supported by a jaw but armed with a complex pattern of horny teeth. Mature males sport a large baggy pouch behind the mouth, the purpose of which is unknown. The round eyes are well developed. A series of seven rounded gill openings lie behind the eyes. There are two dorsal fins at the rear of the body, and a simple caudal fin. Maximum size is 75cm total length.

Distribution in Aotearoa: Widespread around coastal Aotearoa from Te Tai Tokerau Northland to Murihiku Southland, Rakiura Stewart Island and Rēkohu Chatham Island. They can penetrate upriver 230km to an altitude of 380m above sea level. The IUCN lists this species as Data Deficient; however, degradation of lowland waterways and lamprey reddening syndrome has significantly diminished their numbers in Aotearoa.

Habitat: Buried in sand of rivers and streams when juvenile, filter-feeding on organic material. Lamprey need clean waterways with sand and boulders.

Curator's notes: The lamprey was once thought to have the widest natural distribution in the world of any freshwater fish, from southern Australia to Chile, Argentina, Falkland Islands and South Georgia. Closer examination has found the South American fishes to be a different species. On metamorphosis, they run to sea and adopt a 'vampire' lifestyle, feeding on the blood of marine mammals and larger fishes.

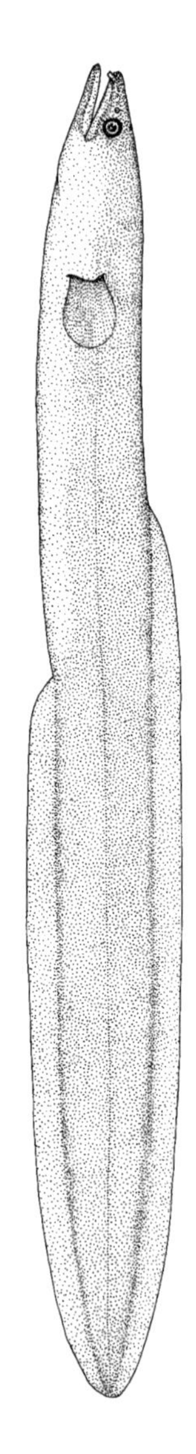

AROKEHE, KOIKOIWHAHA, KŪWHARUWHARU, NGOINGOIWAHA, ŌREA, REHEREHE, TUNA

LONGFIN EEL

Anguilla dieffenbachii

Description: This eel is blue black to dark brown, with a variable belly colour, often depending on the water (clear or tannin stained), ranging from white to a dirty dark yellow. It has the classic eel-shape: elongate, heavy-bodied, cylindrical towards the front and compressed towards the rear. The mouth is large, extending well past the back of the small round eyes, with thick lips. Teeth occur as a broad band of rough, sharp patches on both jaws and the roof of the mouth. The dorsal, caudal and anal fins are continuous, the dorsal starting well before the anal. The pectoral fins are small and rounded. Maximum size is 70cm (males) and 1.75m (females) total length.

Distribution in Aotearoa: An endemic species, widespread throughout both main islands and Rēkohu Wharekauri Chatham Islands in fresh waters except above large rapids, waterfalls and human obstructions (culverts, dams, etc.). It is listed by the IUCN as Endangered. Habitat destruction, overharvesting and climate change are putting this species under increasing pressure.

Habitat: Rivers, streams, lakes and swamps. This species is able to penetrate inland to the most central regions of the country.

Curator's notes: A taonga species, this is the largest and heaviest freshwater eel species in the world. The biggest specimens are females. They move further inland than the males, and they take longer to reach maturity. On maturity, eels run to sea and spawn somewhere around New Caledonia (the specific location has not been confirmed). The longfin eel has suffered from a poor public image; bounties were placed on their destruction from the 1930s to 1960s as they were thought to prey on introduced trout and degrade the fishery. However public attitudes have changed, and they have become a tourist attraction as they can be tamed to be hand-fed. There has been a significant commercial harvest.

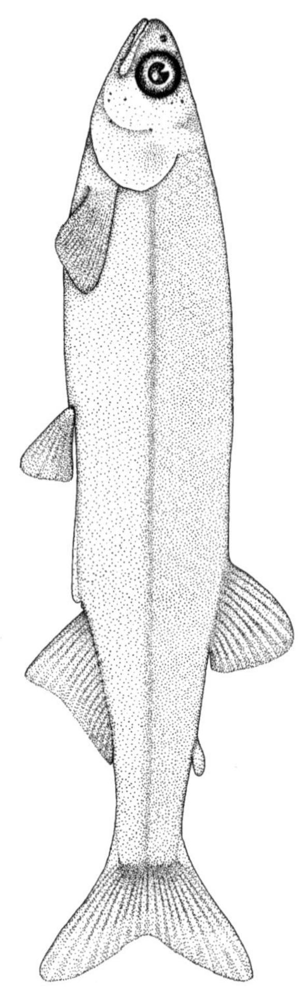

INANGA PAPA, KEHAKEHA, NGAIORE, NGAORE

SMELT

Retropinna retropinna

Description: A bright silver with blue and green iridescent sheens on the back, the smelt has a dark midline stripe and a silvery white belly. Its body is fusiform, with a slightly compressed head and body. The bluntly pointed snout contains a mouth armed with small pointed teeth that extends to almost the back of the large rounded eyes. The dorsal fin is lobate and positioned just past the mid-body, followed by a small adipose fin. The caudal fin is forked, with rounded tine tips. The pectoral fins are low on the body and bluntly pointed. The pelvic fins lie about midway along the body, followed by a low adipose fin. The angular anal fin is positioned below the dorsal fin and is slightly longer. The body is covered with thin deciduous scales. Maximum size is 16.5cm fork length.

Distribution in Aotearoa: An endemic species, widespread throughout Aotearoa including Rakiura Stewart Island and Rēkohu Chatham Island.

Habitat: Found in clean rivers, streams and larger lakes, preferring still to slow-flowing waters. There is a mixture of land-locked and sea-running populations throughout Aotearoa. Sea-running populations can run over 230km inland and to 480m above sea level.

Curator's notes: Although this is not a true smelt, early Europeans thought it was and the name has stuck. A number of land-locked populations were established after being introduced for both food and as prey for introduced trout. Smelt are fairly fast-growing and live for only a couple of years. Sea-running populations return with whitebait, and their strong cucumber smell can taint the whitebait catch. Smelt are important prey species for birds and larger fishes. A second smelt species, Stockell's smelt (*Stokellia anisodon*), is found only in the lower reaches of rivers along the Waitaha Canterbury coast. The te reo names given here are used for adults.

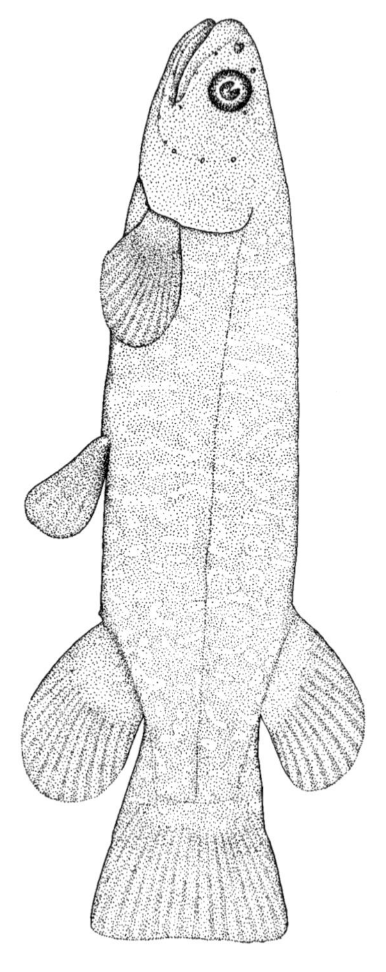

KOKOPARA, TAIWHARU
GIANT KOKOPU

Galaxias argenteus

Description: This fish is dark olive brown to a browning black, and covered with a profusion of golden spots, lines, crescents and rings. Its body is fusiform and its head rounded. The large mouth, armed with large fangs, extends to below about the back edge of the large rounded eyes. The dorsal fin is lobate and positioned just before the caudal fin, which is truncate to emarginate. The pectoral and pelvic fins are both large and lobe-shaped. The anal fin mirrors the dorsal fin and lies opposite it. Maximum size is 58cm fork length.

Distribution in Aotearoa: An endemic species, found around Aotearoa from Te Tai Tokerau Northland to Rakiura Stewart Island, more commonly in the south. The giant kokopu is listed by IUCN as Vulnerable. Harvesting the juveniles as part of the whitebait stock, along with degrading of the preferred habitat of lowland waterways, wetlands and swamps, has put this species under pressure.

Habitat: Prefers slow-flowing streams, lowland lakes with a thick vegetation margin, swamps and wetlands. In spite of its size, the giant kokopu does not penetrate far inland.

Curator's notes: This is the largest galaxiid species in the world, and one of the first to be discovered and named by European explorers. An ambush predator, they take aquatic insects, smelt and any insects landing on the water. It is one of the five species that make up the commercial and recreational catch of whitebait (pages 125–131). Aquarium-kept specimens tend to eat their tankmates. Solitary as adults, they can live for 20 years or more. The maximum weight recorded is 2.7kg. The te reo names given here are used for adults.

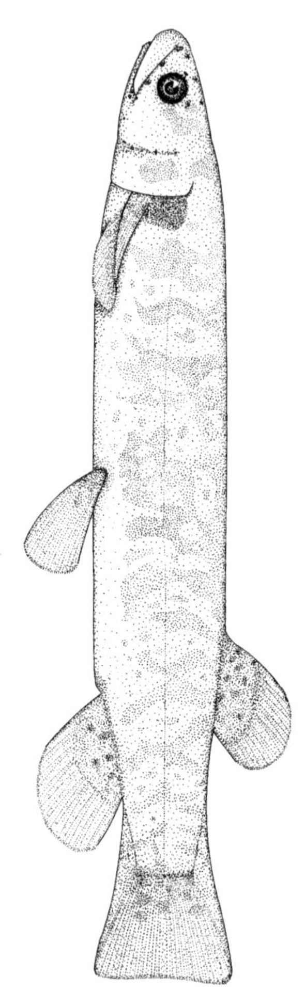

HIWIHIWI, KAKAWAI, KŌWARO, MAEHA, MIROITI, MOHOMOHI, NGOHONGOHO, PANGARE, RĀWAI, RUAMAHEHE, TAIWHARU, TOHITOHI

KŌARO

Galaxias brevipinnis

Description: The kōaro is brown to golden, sometimes grey, with variable darker reticulations, spots and bars. A diffuse dark vertical blotch lies behind the gill, above the pectoral fins. Its body is long, slender and fusiform. The head is slightly depressed. The large mouth extends to the back edge of the small rounded eyes, with the lower jaw hidden under the upper when the mouth is closed. The dorsal fin is lobate and positioned just before the caudal fin, which is truncate to emarginate. The pectoral and pelvic fins are both large and lobate. The anal fin lies slightly behind and mirrors the dorsal fin. Maximum size is 25cm fork length.

Distribution in Aotearoa: Widespread on both main islands. It also occurs on Rakiura Stewart, Rēkohu Wharekauri Chatham, Motu Maha Auckland and Motu Ihupuku Campbell islands.

Habitat: Prefers clean, small to medium-sized streams in native forest with stones, sandy patches and rapids. Kōaro are occasionally seen inland in high-country lakes with an outlet.

Curator's notes: Kōaro are known for their ability to traverse large vertical barriers as long as there is some moisture present on the surface. The pectoral and pelvic fin rays have small flange-like structures extending out on the underside and can be pressed down to act like gecko's feet, giving them good purchase. This way they can 'walk' up a vertical surface in short bursts. The kōaro is also found in south-east Australia. This is another species in the whitebait catch, known as 'jelly bait' because of its somewhat slimy texture. It is the second most important whitebait species in terms of numbers. The te reo names given here are used for adults.

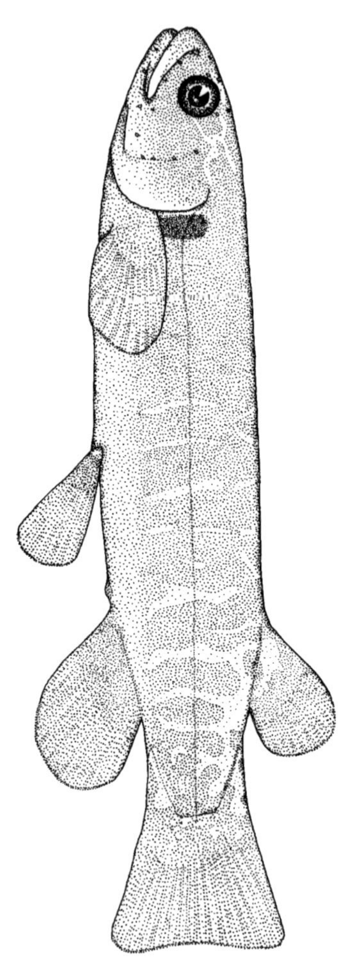

KOKOPU TAIWHARA, KOPU, KŌAWHEAWHE, KŌKOPU, KŌKOPURUAO, KŌPAKOPAKO, KŌRIWHARIWHA, MORURU, PARA, PARAKEKE, RUAO, RUWAO

BANDED KOKOPU

Galaxias fasciatus

Description: The banded kokopu is olive brown to golden, with narrow pale bands often crossing the body and the back of the fish. Diffuse silver and dark vertical blotches occur behind the gill, above the pectoral fins. The body is fusiform and the head rounded. The large mouth, extending to below the back edge of the large rounded eyes, points up slightly and is armed with large fangs. The dorsal fin is lobate and lies just before the caudal fin, which is truncate to emarginate. The large pectoral and pelvic fins are lobate. The anal fin lies opposite and mirrors the dorsal fin but is slightly larger. Maximum size is 26cm fork length.

Distribution in Aotearoa: An endemic species, found throughout Aotearoa including Rakiura Stewart Island and Rēkohu Wharekauri Chatham Islands.

Habitat: Small bush streams with thick vegetation around the margins. It prefers cool water with high tannin levels but has the ability to penetrate up to 177km inland.

Curator's notes: Although solitary, larger pools will support several specimens of a range of sizes. They are superficially similar to the giant kokopu (*Galaxias argenteus*, page 125), but differ in the narrow pale bars that cross the back. They can be easily seen if the observer sits quietly by a pool and flicks worms or small bits of bread into the water. Banded kokopu adapt quite well to being kept in aquaria as long as the water temperature can be kept down. Numbers have declined in many regions where forest cover has been removed. Juveniles make up another of the whitebait species. The te reo names given here are used for adults.

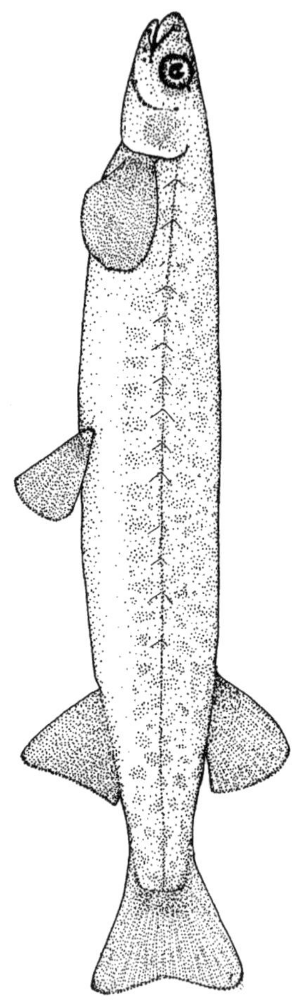

HIWI, KARAHI
INANGA

Galaxias maculatus

Description: This fish is translucent golden to greenish with scattered darker spots and a silvery white belly. A swim bladder is visible through the gut wall. Its body is slender and fusiform with a small tapering head. The small mouth does not extend past the middle of the large eyes. The dorsal fin is lobate and positioned just before the caudal fin; the latter is truncate to emarginate. Both the pectoral and pelvic fins are large and lobate. The slightly angular anal fin lies opposite the dorsal fin and is a little longer. Maximum size is 19cm fork length.

Distribution in Aotearoa: Around coastal Aotearoa including Rakiura Stewart Island and Rēkohu Wharekauri Chatham Islands. Although listed by the IUCN as Least Concern, habitat destruction and overfishing of whitebait suggests that numbers are declining. Riparian restoration by planting native vegetation, and fencing stock away from river margins, has seen increases in numbers.

Habitat: Found in larger, slow-flowing rivers and streams as well as in coastal lakes, and larger pools in native forest.

Curator's notes: Inanga form large schools in the midwater of rivers and large streams. Being very skittish, any movement will cause the school to scatter, then quickly reform. Their prey is small insect larvae. This is the largest and most important component of the five galaxiid species that make up the whitebait catch. Inanga is the most widespread member of the Galaxiidae family, and one of the most widely naturally distributed freshwater fishes in the world. As well as Aotearoa, they are found around south Australia, Tasmania, Lord Howe Island, southern South America and the Falkland Islands.

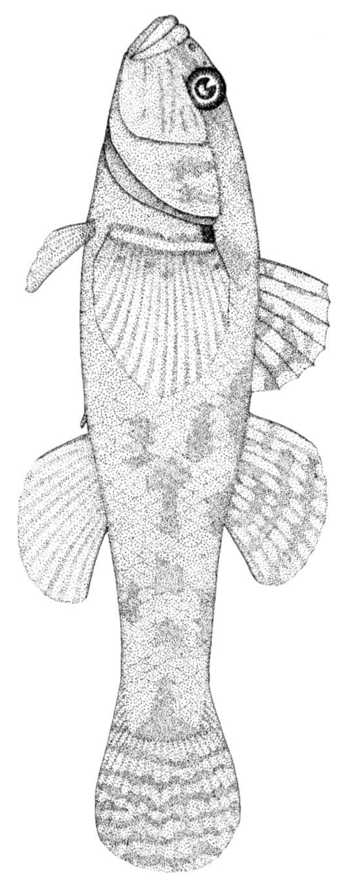

TĪPOKOPOKO, TOITOI
COMMON BULLY

Gobiomorphus cotidianus

Description: The common bully is mottled brown and tan, with mature males being darker. Its body is stout, rounded towards the front and compressed towards the rear. The head is bluntly pointed. The mouth is tilted up and extends to the front of the round eyes that sit high on the head. The first dorsal fin has seven to eight slender spines, the second has a single spine and 9 to 10 soft rays. The caudal fin is lobate. The pectoral fins have a very broad lobe-shape, while the pelvic fins are small and short, positioned directly below. The anal fin lies opposite the second dorsal fin and is about the same shape and size. Maximum size is 15.8cm total length.

Distribution in Aotearoa: Endemic, this fish occurs throughout the country including Rakiura Stewart, Aotea Great Barrier and Rēkohu Wharekauri Chatham islands.

Habitat: Found in rivers, streams and lakes, generally in more coastal and lowland areas but able to penetrate over 300km inland. Some lake populations appear to have been introduced.

Curator's notes: As the common name implies, this is the most frequently encountered of the freshwater bullies, but it wasn't recognised as distinct until 1962, and was only finally scientifically described in 1975. Juveniles run to sea for a period before returning to fresh waters. These juveniles can be included in whitebait catches and have sometimes been called 'whale feed'. Some lake populations are landlocked and do not run to sea. Males guard a nest of eggs deposited on the undersides of rocks. The common bully is an important prey species for eels, trout, herons and shags.

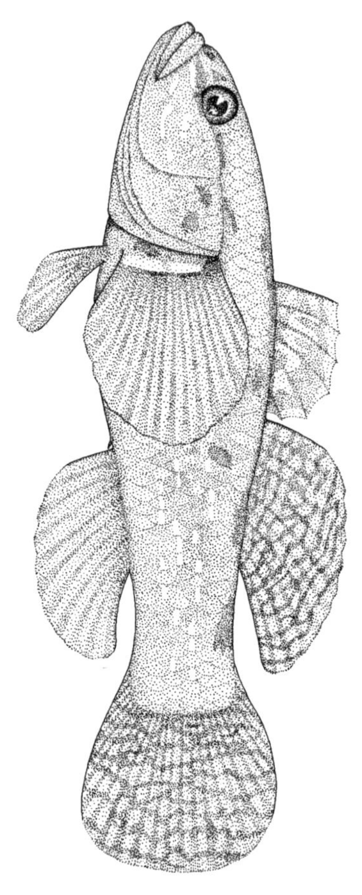

HAWAI, KOKOPU, TOITOI
GIANT BULLY

Gobiomorphus gobioides

Description: The giant bully is mottled dark and mid-brown with bronze flecks. Its body is stout, rounded towards the front and compressed towards the rear. The head is bluntly pointed. The mouth is tilted up and has a protruding lower jaw; it extends to below the front edge of the round eyes that sit high on the head. The first dorsal fin has six slender spines, and the second has a single spine and 9 to 10 soft rays. The caudal fin is lobate. The pectoral fins have a very broad lobe-shape, while the pelvic fins, positioned underneath, are small and short. The anal fin is similar in shape and size to the second dorsal fin and lies opposite it. Maximum size is 24cm total length.

Distribution in Aotearoa: Endemic, with a patchy but widespread distribution around the country. It is not recorded from Rakiura Stewart Island or Rēkohu Wharekauri Chatham Islands. Listed by the IUCN as Least Concern, but given that this species is almost exclusively found in the lower reaches of rivers and coastal wetlands, it is at risk from pollution, habitat degradation and loss.

Habitat: Coastal, rarely seen more than 2km inland, in streams, estuaries, coastal lagoons and swamps.

Curator's notes: When small, this species is often confused with the common bully (*Gobiomorphus cotidianus*, page 133). Despite its large size, the giant bully does not penetrate far inland, much like the giant kokopu. Usually solitary, they hide under overhanging banks and logs, coming out at night to feed. Because of the challenges of working in its preferred habitat, this species has not been well studied.

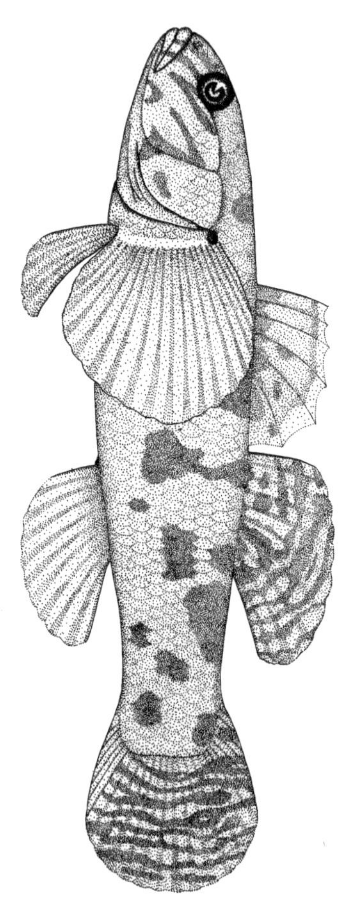

KOPU, TOITOI
RED GILLED BULLY

Gobiomorphus huttoni

Description: Males have bright red patches on the gill cover, blotches along the flank and diagonal lines across the dorsal fins. Females have the same pattern but in brown. Both sexes have diagonal stripes across the cheeks and gill covers. The body is stout, rounded towards the front and compressed towards the rear. The head is bluntly pointed. The mouth, which is tilted up, extends to below the front edge of the round eyes, which sit high on the head. The first dorsal fin has six slender spines, the second a single spine and 9 to 10 soft rays. The caudal fin is lobate. The pectoral fins are a very broad lobe-shape, and the pelvic fins are small and short and positioned below it. The anal fin lies opposite the second dorsal fin, and is similar in size and shape. Maximum size is 12cm total length.

Distribution in Aotearoa: An endemic species, widespread around the country, including Rakiura Stewart Island, Aotea Great Barrier Island and Rēkohu Wharekauri Chatham Islands. Listed by the IUCN as Near Threatened. Degradation of lowland waterways has reduced available habitat and risks the species entering a negative spiral of recruitment and spawning.

Habitat: Found in rivers and streams with swift flows and boulders. This species is capable of penetrating up to 266km inland, and to 400m above sea level.

Curator's notes: The males of this species are our most colourful native freshwater fish and have a somewhat enlarged second dorsal fin and blunter snout.

GLOSSARY

REFERENCES AND FURTHER READING

ACKNOWLEDGEMENTS

INDEX OF SPECIES

ABOUT THE AUTHOR

ABOUT THE ILLUSTRATORS

GLOSSARY

Terms that are defined elsewhere in this glossary are shown in italics. The diagrams on pages 12 and 13 are also useful for identifying basic anatomy and units of measurement.

Adipose fin A small lobe-like fin lacking any supporting *spines* or *rays*.

Barbels Sensitive fleshy outgrowths on the head that can detect movement and chemicals produced by prey.

Benthic Living on or under the sea bed.

Caudal fin Tail *fin*. For shapes, see *emarginate, double emarginate, lunate* and *truncate*.

Compressed Flattened from side to side.

Deciduous Easily shed, like leaves in autumn.

Degraded Losing quality because of pollution, silting, etc.

Denticles Tooth-like scales found on the skin of sharks.

Depressed Flattened from top to bottom.

Disc Fused head, trunk and paired fins of some fishes, particularly skates and rays. The disc is measured in width.

Distal Outer part or area.

Dorsal Occurring on or along the upper region of a fish.

Double emarginate Describing a *caudal fin* where the margin has two dips just before the tips and extends slightly in the central region, looking like a 'W' on its side.

ECS Extended Continental Shelf – 200 nautical miles from the continental shelf margin. For Aotearoa, this adds an additional 1,700,000km^2 to the EEZ. The jurisdiction covers only the sea bed and what lies under it.

EEZ Extended Economic Zone – 200 nautical miles from the mean high-water line where we have jurisdiction over both living and non-living resources. For Aotearoa, this amounts to over 4,400,000km^2.

Emarginate Describing a *caudal fin* with a slightly concave, indented or forked edge.

Epipelagic Living in the upper 50m of the open ocean.

Falcate Pointed like a peregrine falcon's wing.

Filament Thread-like appendage.

Fin Structure used for propelling or steering, supported by *spines* and/or *rays*.

Flanks The sides of the fish.

Fork length The distance from the snout to the middle (fork) of the *caudal fin*, often abbreviated as FL.

Fusiform Torpedo-shaped.

Gill rakers Hard, slender structures on the gill arch that project into the mouth cavity. They protect the delicate gill filaments as well as sometimes sieving out prey from the water.

Globose Having the form of a globe, spherical.

Ichthyologist A scientist who studies fishes.

Intertidal Region between the high and low extremes of the tides.

IUCN International Union for the Conservation of Nature.
An international organisation that tracks and provides information about extinction risks of animals, plants and fungi.

Lateral line Line of pored or tubed scales that run along the side of the body that sense vibrations in the water.

Lobe, lobate Rounded projection; describing *fins*, lobe-shaped.

Lunate Describing a *caudal fin* with an inward-curved margin like a crescent moon.

Motu A te reo word for land or island.

Pākehā A te reo word for non-Māori, usually European, or of European ancestry.

Papillae Small fleshy outgrowths.

Pelagic Living in the surface waters.

Ray Flexible, usually segmented structure that supports a *fin* (see also *spine*).

Riparian The margins of rivers, streams and other waterways.

Sea chest A large rectangular indentation of the hull of cargo vessels, used to draw in water to cool the engines and for making fresh water.

Scutes Enlarged, hardened scales, especially found along the rear *lateral line* or along the belly midline in some fishes.

Shell hash Broken and empty shells layered on the sea bed.

Spine Pointed thickened bony structure, sometimes supporting a *fin*, usually unsegmented.

Standard length The length from the tip of the upper jaw to the end of the backbone (seen as a slight fold at the base of the tail), often abbreviated as SL.

Subtidal Region below the low tide mark.

Swim bladder Gas-filled sac positioned beneath the backbone that aids buoyancy.

Te Ika-a-Maūi The te reo name for the North Island, meaning the 'fish of Māui'.

Te Waipounamu The te reo name for the South Island, meaning the 'waters of greenstone'.

Tilly bones Thickened bones named after the German-American palaeontologist Johanna 'Tilly' Edinger.

Total length From the tip of the snout to the tip of the *caudal fin*, often abbreviated as TL.

Truncate Describing a *caudal fin* with a straight edge.

Ventral Occurring on or along the belly region of a fish.

REFERENCES AND FURTHER READING

Andrew, N and M Francis (eds), *The Living Reef: The Ecology of New Zealand's Rocky Reefs*, Craig Potton Publishing, Nelson, 2003.

Barraud, N, *Mangō: Sharks and Rays of Aotearoa*, Te Papa Press, Wellington, 2023.

Caiger, P, *Fishes of Aotearoa*, Potton & Burton, Nelson, 2023.

Carson, S and R Morris, *The New Zealand Seashore Guide*, Potton & Burton, Nelson, 2022.

Francis, M, *Coastal Fishes of New Zealand: A Comprehensive Guide to Identification and Behaviour*, Potton & Burton, Nelson, 2024.

McDowall, RM, *New Zealand Freshwater Fishes: A Natural History and Guide*, Heinemann Reed, Auckland, 1989.

McDowall, RM, *The Reed Field Guide to New Zealand Freshwater Fishes*, Reed Books, Auckland, 2000.

McDowall, RM, *Ikawai: Freshwater Fishes in Māori Culture and Economy*, Canterbury University Press, Christchurch, 2011.

McMillan, PJ *et al.*, 'New Zealand fishes: A field guide to common species caught by bottom, midwater, and surface fishing', *New Zealand Aquatic Environment and Biodiversity Report*, no. 208, 2019, mpi.govt.nz/dmsdocument/34632/direct (accessed 16 May 2025).

McQueen, S, *A Photographic Guide to Freshwater Fishes of New Zealand*, New Holland, Auckland, 2013.

McQueen, S, *The New Zealand Native Freshwater Aquarium*, Upstart Press / New Holland, Auckland, 2018.

Morton, J, *Seashore Ecology of New Zealand and the Pacific*, David Bateman, Auckland, 2004.

Mossman, S, *Snapper: New Zealand's Greatest Fish: Te Ika Rangatira o Aotearoa*, AUT Media, Auckland, 2008.

Nelson, JS, *Fishes of the World* (3rd edition), John Wiley & Sons, New York, 1994.

Paulin, C and C Roberts, *The Rockpool Fishes of New Zealand: Te Ika Āria o Aotearoa*, Southwestern Publishing, Auckland, 1992.

Phillipps, WJ, *Native Fishes of New Zealand*, AH & AW Reed, Wellington, 1949.

Roberts, CD, AL Stewart and CD Struthers (eds), *The Fishes of New Zealand* (four volumes), Te Papa Press, Wellington, 2015.

Strickland, RR, 'Nga tini a Tangaroa: A Maori–English, English–Maori dictionary of fish names', *New Zealand Fisheries Occasional Publication*, no. 5, 1990, pp. 1–60.

Vennell, R, *Secrets of the Sea: The Story of New Zealand's Native Sea Creatures*, HarperCollins, Auckland, 2022.

ACKNOWLEDGEMENTS

This book has been distilled from a lifetime's passion for fishes and the incredible privilege I have had to have known and worked with some of the great ichthyologists of the twentieth century. In addition, I have to say a grateful thank you to my parents, Rex and Marie, who supported my unusual fascination, and my wife, Liz, who acquiesced to my standard reply to 'What do you want for Christmas / your birthday?' with 'Something with a fish on it, or something with a fish in it.'

Many thanks to my colleague Carl Struthers, Transition Manager at Te Papa, for his peer review of this book. Thanks to Publisher Michael Upchurch and Project Editors Olive Owens and Olivia Nikkel at Te Papa Press. Thanks to Tim Denee for the series design, Sarah Elworthy for typesetting, Teresa McIntrye for editing, Emily Goldthorpe and Olive Owens for proofreading and Jo Elliott and Sophia Walsh for indexing.

INDEX OF SPECIES

Bold page numbers refer to species descriptions.

A

Acanthoclinus fuscus **55**
Ahuruhuru **51**
Aldrichetta forsteri **57**
Allomycterus pilatus **113**
Anguilla dieffenbachii **121**
Aplodactylus arctidens **79**
Arara **63**
Arāra **63**
Arokehe **121**
Arripis
  trutta 57, **69**
  xylabion 69
Aua **57**
Awa **57**

B

Banded kokopu **129**
Banded wrasse **101**
Bathytoshia brevicaudata **29**
Bellapiscis medius **91**
Blue cod 9, **109**
Blue moki 14, **73**
Bothidae (family) 59
Bully
  common **133**, 135
  giant **135**
  red gilled **137**
Burrfish, southern **113**
Butterfish **97**

C

Carpet shark **21**
Cephaloscyllium isabellum **21**
Cheeseman' puffer 115
Chelidonichthys kumu **45**
Chirodactylus spectabilis **75**
Chrysophrys auratus **71**
Clingfish, orange **87**, *89*
Cod
  blue 9, **109**
  northern bastard 41
  red **39**, 41, 61
  rock **37**, 39
  southern bastard 14, **41**
Common bully **133**, *135*
Common sole **61**
Common triplefin *7*, *10*, **93**
Conger eel **31**
Conger verreauxi **31**
Copper moki 53
Cryptic hagfish **19**

D

Diplocrepus punaceus **87**, 89

E

Eagle ray **27**, 29
Eel
  conger **31**
  longfin **121**
Ehouhouamu **75**
Eptatretus cryptus **19**
Eyebrow perch 53

F

Flounder, yellowbelly **59**, 61
Forsterygion
  lapillum **93**
  varium **95**

G

Gaidropsarus novaezealandiae **43**
Galaxias
  argenteus **125**, 129
  brevipinnis **127**
  fasciatus **129**
  maculatus **131**

Galaxiidae (family) 131
Genyagnus monopterygius **107**
Geotria australis **119**
Giant boarfish 14, **67**
Giant bully **135**
Giant kokopu **125**, 129
Girella tricuspidate **77**
Goatfish **51**
Gobiomorphus
  cotidianus **133**, 135
  gobioides **135**
  huttoni **137**
Gonorynchus forsteri **35**
Gurnard, red **45**

H
Haku **65**
Hāpukupuku **69**
Hawai **135**
Helicolenus percoides **85**
Hemerocoetes monopterygius **81**
Hinamoki **47**
Hippocampus abdominalis **47**, 49
Hirihiri **117**
Hiwi **131**
Hiwihiwi **127**
Hoka **39**
Hoodwinker sunfish **111**
Hypoplectrodes
  sp A 53
  Hypoplectrodes huntii **53**

I
Inanga **131**
Inanga papa **123**

J
Jock stewart **85**

K
Kahawai 11,14, 57, **69**
Kahu **65**
Kakawai **127**
Kanakana **119**
Kanakana-wairaki **119**
Kapetā **25**
Karahi **131**
Karatī **71**
Kātaha **57**
Kataka **57**
Katirimu **79**
Kawikawi **79**
Kehakeha **123**
Kehe **79**
Keke **79**
Kingfish **65**
Kiore moana **47**
Kiore waitai **47**
Kirirī **117**
Kōaro **127**
Kōawheawhe **129**
Koeae **79**
Kōeaea **97**
Kōhere **69**
Kohikohi **81**
Koiero **31**
Koikoiwhaha **121**
Koinga **23**
Kōiro **31**
Kōkiri **117**
Kokirikiri **117**
Kokopara 125
Kokopu **135**
Kokopu
  banded **129**
  giant **125**
Kōkopu **129**
Kokopu taiwhara **129**
Kōkopuruao **129**
Komutumutu **63**
Kōpakopako **129**
Kopapa **63**, **69**
Kopīpiro 77
Kopu **129**, **137**
Kōpūhuri **69**
Kopukopu **109**
Kōpūtōtara **113**
Kōpūwaitōtara **113**
Koria **69**

Kōriro **31**
Kōriwhariwha **129**
Korokoro **119**
Kouarea **71**
Kōukauka **69**
Kourea **71**
Kourepoua **107**
Kōwaitau **69**
Kōwaro **127**
Kōwerewere **69**
Kumukumu **45**
Kūngongingongi **69**
Kutuhori **61**
Kūwharuwharu **121**

L

Lagocephalus cheesemanii **115**
Lamprey **119**
Latridopsis
  cilaris **73**
  forsteri **73**
Leatherjacket **117**
Longfin eel **121**
Lotella rhacina **37**, 39
Lumpfish **89**

M

Maeha **127**
Makawhiti **57**
Makumaku **65**
Manaia **47**
Mangā **25**
Mangō **25**
Mangō-hapū **23**
Mangō-pekepeke **23**
Manua **75**
Māori chief **105**
Marahea **57**
Marare **97**
Marari **97**
Mararī **97**
Maratea **75**
Maratia **75**
Maraua **57**
Marblefish **79**
Matakā **57**
Matakawhiti **57**
Matohe **97**
Matuawhapuku **85**
Meuschenia scaber **117**
Miroiti **127**
Moamoa **107**
Mōhakihaki **89**
Mohiaru **89**
Mohimohi **33**
Mohomohi **127**
Moki **73**
Moki
  blue 14, **73**
  copper 73
  red **75**
Mokowhiti **57**
Mola
  alexandrini 111
  mola 111
  tecta **111**
Moruru **129**
Mōwhakiwhaki **89**
Mullet
  red **51**
  yelloweye 7, **57**
Muritea **77**
Mustelus lenticulatus **25**
Myliobatis tenuicaudatus **27**, 29

N

Nanua **75**
Nanua pounamu **75**
Napia **19**
Ngaiore **123**
Nganangana **119**
Ngāoheohe **77**
Ngaore **123**
Ngehe **79**
Ngohongoho **127**
Ngoingoi **31**
Ngoingoiwaha **121**
Ngoio **31**

Ngōiro **31**
Ngu **107**
Ngutere **75**
Nohu **113**
Northern bastard cod **41**
Notolabrus
    celidotus **99**, 101
    fucicola **101**
Notothenia angustata **105**

O
Odax pullus **97**
Olive rockfish **55**
Opalfish **81**
Orange clingfish **87**, 89
Ōrea **121**
Oru **29**

P
Paekirikiri **99**
Pākau **29**
Pākaurua **29**
Pakeke **61**
Paketi **99**
Pakirikiri **99**
Pākirikiri **109**
Pangare **127**
Para **129**
Parakeke **129**
Parakoka **7**
Parapercis colias **109**
Paratete **71**
Paratohe **71**
Partistiopterus labiosus **67**
Patatī **71**
Pātiki tōtara **59**
Pātōtara **59**
Pātutuki **109**
Pātiki rore **61**
Pātiki rori **61**
Pau **103**
Pawaiwhakarua **103**
Pekapeka **21**
Peltorhamphus novaezeelandiae **61**
Pepe tamure **71**
Perch
    eyebrow 53
    red-banded **53**
Pia **19**, **119**
Pihapiharau **119**
Piharu **119**
Pilchard **33**
Pinguipedidae (family) 109
Pioke **25**
Pipiharau **119**
Pohuiakaroa **85**
Pohuikaroa **85**
Pōnaho **57**
Porore **77**
Pseudocaranx georgianus **63**, 69, 71
Pseudolabrus miles **103**
Pseudophycis
    bachus **39**, 41
    barbata **41**
    breviuscula 41
Puaihakarua 85
Pūawai 69
Puhikorokoro 119
Pūwaiwhakarua 103
Pūwhaiau **45**

R
Rarī **97**
Rātāhuihui **111**
Ratutu **59**
Raumarie ārāra **63**
Raumarire **63**
Raumarie **63**
Raututu **61**
Rāwai **127**
Rāwaru **109**
Red cod **39**, 41, 61
Red gilled bully **137**
Red gurnard **45**
Red moki **75**
Red mullet **51**
Red-banded perch **53**
Reherehe **121**

Retropinna retropinna **123**
Rhombosolea leporine **59**, 61
Rig **25**
Rock cod **37**, 39
Rockfish, olive **55**
Rockling **43**
Roha **29**
Ruamahehe **127**
Ruamarie **63**
Ruamarie ārāra **63**
Ruao **129**
Ruwao **129**

S
Sandfish **35**
Sardinops sagax **33**
Scarlet wrasse **103**
Scorpaena papillosa **83**, 85
Scorpionfish 14, **83**, 85
Seahorse **47**, 49
Seriola lalandi **65**
Shorttail stingray **29**
Smelt **123**, 125
Smooth pipefish **49**
Snapper **71**
Southern bastard cod 14, **41**
Southern burrfish **113**
Spiny dogfish **23**, 25
Spotted stargazer **107**
Spotty 7, **99**, 101
Squalus acanthias **23**, 25
Stigmatophora macropterygia **49**
Stockell's smelt 123
Stokellia anisodon 123

T
Tāhuri **69**
Taiwharu **125**, **127**
Tāmure **71**
Tāngahangaha **99**, **101**
Tāngāngā **99**
Tapurupuru **69**
Tarao **97**
Tarore **61**
Tāroto **69**
Taumaka **55**
Tīpokopoko **133**
Tohitohi **127**
Toitoi **133**, **135**, **137**
Totoke **31**
Trachelochismus pinnulatus **89**
Trevally **63**, 69, 71
Triplefin
  common 7,10, 93
  twister 7, 10, 91
  variable 7, 10, **95**
Tripterygion capito **93**
Tuare **19**
Tuere **19**
Tuna **121**
Tuna korokoro **119**
Twister 7, 10, **91**

U
Upenichthys porosus **51**
Ute **119**

V
Variable triplefin 7, 10, **95**

W
Wairaki **119**
Waituere **119**
Warehenga **65**
Whai **29**
Whai repo **27**, **29**
Whaiwhai **59**
Wrasse
  banded **101**
  scarlet **103**

Y
Yellowbelly flounder **59**, 61
Yelloweye mullet 7, **57**

ABOUT THE AUTHOR

Andrew Stewart got hooked on fishes at about age three and announced at five that he was going to be a fish scientist. Starting at the (then) National Museum as Technician of Fishes in 1982, over the last 43 years he has accumulated a broad base of knowledge about fishes from fresh water to marine, coastal to deep sea and subtropical to the Antarctic. He is currently Curator Vertebrates at Te Papa. His particular love is of the deep-water fishes, especially female anglerfishes with their unique lures and mouths full of gigantic teeth, which he refers to as 'lovely girls'.

ABOUT THE ILLUSTRATORS

HELEN CASEY

Helen completed a degree in Visual Communication Design from Wellington Polytech, and was initially employed by the Dominion Museum in 1990 as an illustrator for *The Rockpool Fishes of New Zealand* (published in 1992). She was kept on to illustrate New Zealand and New Caledonian fish species. Several of these were used in new species descriptions. In total, Helen produced 171 drawings. She left the museum in 1996 to pursue private commercial illustration work.

MICHELLE FREEBORN

Michelle was the longest-serving fishes illustrator at Te Papa, starting in January 2002. Although officially finishing in November 2014 (with the publication of *The Fishes of New Zealand* in 2015), Michelle has been retained on contract, and one of her illustrations of a new species of dragonfish was published as recently as 2023. Over her twelve years at Te Papa, Michelle produced 1358 drawings, almost all of New Zealand species with some Antarctic snailfishes.

ERIKA MACKAY

Erika trained in Graphic Design at Wellington Polytech and replaced Helen Casey as an illustrator at Te Papa in July 1996. She was illustrator until October 2001, when she left to take up a position at the National Institute of Water and Atmospheric Research (NIWA). Erika returned in 2010 to do one contract drawing for a paper on Antarctic snailfishes. Over the time she was at Te Papa, she produced 444 drawings, almost exclusively of New Zealand marine fishes.

BOB MCDOWALL

Bob was the 'dean of freshwater fishes' for Aotearoa New Zealand. Over the course of his 48-year career as a freshwater fisheries scientist he published over 200 scientific papers, over 300 scientific reports, numerous popular articles, and 14 books. The latter were the first comprehensive guides to our native freshwater fishes. As well as his prodigious publication outputs, Bob was also a skilled illustrator, and some of these illustrations have been utilised here. Sadly, Bob passed away in 2011.

First published in New Zealand in 2025 by
Te Papa Press, PO Box 467, Wellington, New Zealand
www.tepapapress.co.nz

A catalogue record is available from the National Library
of New Zealand

978-1-99-107212-2

Cover and internal design by Tim Denee
Cover illustrations based on the snapper (*Chrysophrys auratus*), eagle ray (*Myliobatis tenuicaudatus*) and kahawai (*Arripis trutta*)
Typesetting by Sarah Elworthy
Digital imaging by Yoan Jolly

Printed by Everbest Printing Investment Limited